The word Yiribana means 'this way'

It derives from the Eora language, spoken by the original people of Sydney

YIRIBANA

An introduction to the

Aboriginal and Torres Strait Islander Collection
The Art Gallery of New South Wales

by Margo Neale

CONTENTS

The publication of this book coincides with the opening of the new gallery of Aboriginal art – Yiribana. It is, therefore, a two-fold celebration; firstly, a timely and representative publication of highlights from the Aboriginal collection of this Gallery and, secondly, the opening of a wonderful and inspiring new facility that will allow the Gallery to properly and imaginatively display and contribute to the evolving traditions of Aboriginal art and culture. The Yiribana gallery is the largest single space devoted to the permanent exhibition of Aboriginal and Torres Strait Islander art and culture in the world. Its opening is a most significant milestone in the history of this Gallery and it pays due recognition, not only to the great and known traditions of Aboriginal art that are so exemplified in the Gallery's marvellous holding of bark paintings, but also to the new dynamism of contemporary Aboriginal art practice now being expressed in both urban and rural communities.

Body design on young boys.
Photo Penny Tweedie Nangalala N.T. 1979

Even though this collection began in the 1950s, it is, in fact the first major survey publication of our collection. It is intended to meet the needs of a growing number of international visitors to this Gallery as well as our Australian audiences who seek a greater understanding and appreciation of the art of the original Australians. It makes a valuable contribution to the way we look at Aboriginal art today and provides insights into the distinctive values and attitudes of Aboriginal cultural traditions. The documentation and publication of our collection in this form, in particular our classic barks, is something to which we have aspired for some time.

I thank Margo Neale, the author, a person of Aboriginal and Irish descent, and our Aboriginal Curator, Daphne Wallace of the Gamilaroi group in New South Wales for all their work in realising this publication. In particular, Margo Neale has brought to this book a gifted eye informed by her direct experience with Aboriginal art in the out-stations of Arnhem Land during the 1970s and her continuing experience in bringing Aboriginal art to a wider audience.

Like all such endeavours this book, and indeed the Yiribana gallery, is a collaborative effort. None of this would have been achieved without the full commitment of the Gallery's Department of Australian art. To all those associated with the book and the Yiribana gallery we express our thanks for making possible these events that are truly in the spirit of reconciliation, and a clear demonstration of The Art Gallery of New South Wales commitment to the art of the original Australians.

Edmund Capon

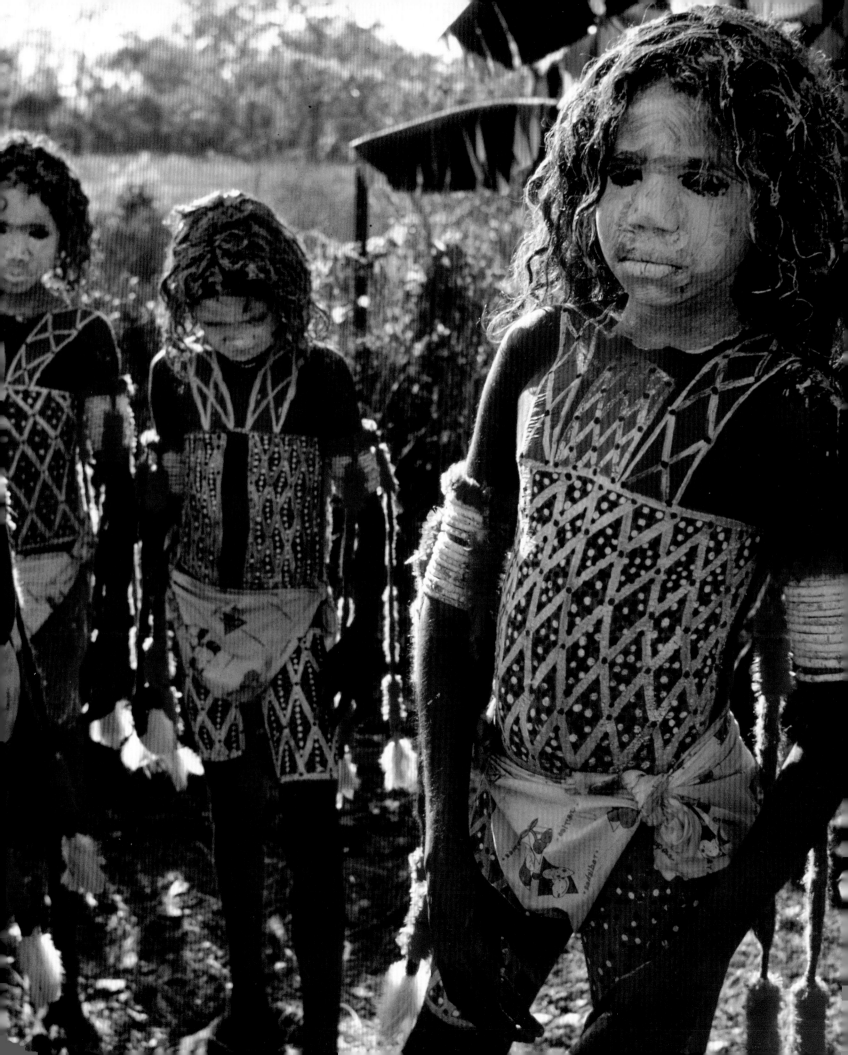

For more than four decades, The Art Gallery of New South Wales has been collecting works of Aboriginal and Torres Strait Islander art. The purpose of this book and of the Yiribana Gallery, which its publication celebrates, is to introduce this collection to a wider public. Though strongly focused on the present day, the selection of works demonstrates both the quality and the historical scope of the Gallery's acquisitions over the years.

The Gallery's collection reflects not only the dynamic growth of indigenous art in this country over the past half century, but also the cultural stereotyping which has often been its burden. This book sets out to challenge some of these stereotypes and expand viewers' perceptions of this constantly evolving art. Aboriginal and Torres Strait Islander art today is a vital contemporary art form which is diverse and constantly changing. It is meant to be viewed, read and shared – and refuses to be narrowly defined.

Ceremony about Macassan contact. Dancers from Groote Eylandt and Numbulwar use flags to represent the sails of Macassan praus.
Photo Penny Tweedie Nangala N.T. 1979

The selection of works has been organised around seven themes which depart significantly from earlier divisions of Aboriginal art into geographical regions, or different media, or chronological sequence. Most of the seven sections encompass a range of works from different regions, time periods and media designed to show conceptual links, the persistence of 'Aboriginality', and the adaptability of Aboriginal artists to new ideas and materials. Because of the multi-referential nature of much Aboriginal art, a number of works selected for one theme could be equally comfortable under several others. With the current proliferation of Aboriginal art-making, its amazing diversity and the mobility of artists today, it was felt that the themes chosen make accessible the Gallery's collection in a contemporary context.

Contemporary Traditional

Until recently, many people regarded bark paintings as the only 'authentic' Aboriginal art form: relics of another age, frozen in time. [1] From this now out-dated perspective, the use of non-traditional materials and art styles could not be 'real' Aboriginal art. [2] Yet these same people would accept that artists in other cultures and other periods of history have always responded to their environment and used the materials available to them. Renaissance artists used ochres and oxides to depict 'creation stories' on wood panels just as Aboriginal artists from Arnhem Land did on bark – and do today. As oil paint and other media became accessible, European artists in the seventeenth and eighteenth centuries started portraying less traditional themes on new surfaces like canvas, glass and paper in much the same way Aboriginal artists with access to new materials do today. Some artists from urban and rural areas, no longer living on their own land, also use traditional motifs to express their personal concerns, to interrogate and re-write history, to affirm their Aboriginality and to stake their claim to a place in history.

While style and region often concur, it is also necessary to recognise artistic exchanges – between desert, 'Top End' and urban artists – and the cultural influences and collaborations with non-Aboriginal artists which occur. The so-called 'urban' style was initially practiced primarily by Aboriginal artists living in urban and outlying rural regions who have been most affected by white contact and have varying degrees of access to their own cultural traditions as well as to the traditions of other cultures. A sense of their Aboriginality strongly informs their work. [3]

'Traditional' artists come from regions less disrupted by the invaders and urbanisation, and are able to draw on often unbroken cultural

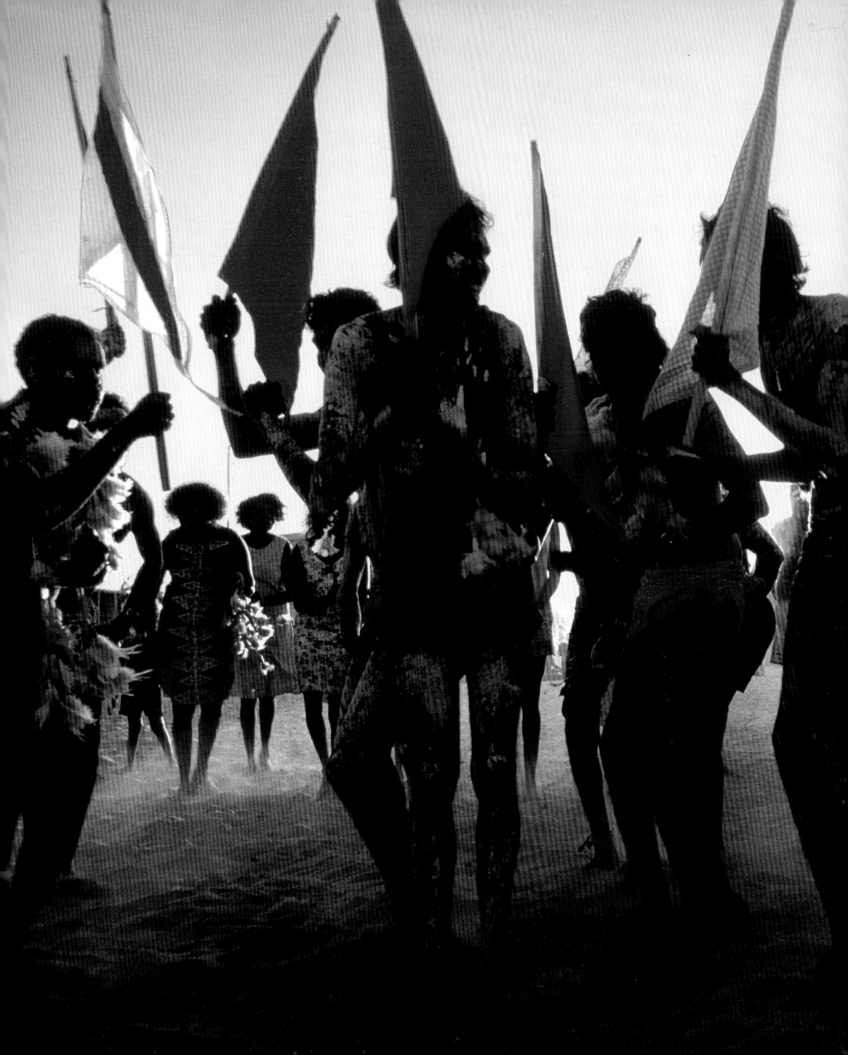

Right top
Artist Unknown
Macassan Prau
c1948
Plate 1

Right bottom
Artist Unknown
Sydney Harbour Bridge
1939
Plate 2

"On Milingimbi, in the Crocodile Island group off the coast of Arnhem Land, old man Djawa, the undisputed 'boss' of the Gupapuyngu people whose word was 'law', would tell me stories about the Macassan trepang fisherman who 'lived' with them long ago. As we sat under the line of grand tamarind trees planted by the Macassans, he would jerk his head topped by a massive crop of white hair and thrust his chin forward in the direction of the Island of Rapuma nearby and tell of the women who used to camp with them there. In the 1970s I saw many people who were the legacy of these unions, even generations later."

Margo Neale

traditions. Increasingly, however they have mobility and access to new ideas and materials and innovate within these flexible traditions. Old and continuing stories are often reworked and transferred to new mediums just as, for example, the Garden of Eden, or other Christian themes are continually represented in new mediums by European (and Aboriginal) artists.

In this book, the terms 'traditional' and 'urban' are attempts to capture the source or inspiration of two different styles of work being done by Aboriginal artists today. 'Traditional' does not mean something old and unchanging – a static art form which is simply copied into the present for nostalgic or other reasons. Nor does 'urban art' mean that artists who work in 'non-traditional' styles have no cultural traditions or that they live necessarily in cities or towns. They are both contemporary art practices. "The labels of 'traditional' and 'urban' are clearly unsatisfactory for they take no account of the 'open borders' between desert, regional and urban artists."[4] It is increasingly anomalous to locate Aboriginal artists regionally in an art world that does not define non-Aboriginal artists primarily by region of origin or residence.

One strong tradition of Aboriginal art which is often overlooked is its consistent responsiveness to contact with other cultures. To believe that Aboriginal art before the advent of Europeans was completely 'uncontaminated' contradicts the visual and historic evidence. Ancient drawings of various kinds of boats from Indonesia, as well as images of fair-skinned foreigners (see plate 4) may be still found on rock walls. Macassan praus (fishing boats) from Sulawesi, Sama-Bajau craft (Lanung) and the long canoes of Maluku appeared in rock art for centuries and continued to do so in the bark paintings of Groote Eylandt artists until the 1960s.[5] The dugout canoe, the wet weather platform houses of Arnhem Land and the pipe are legacies of this

contact. A number of important ceremonies incorporate Macassan activities and symbols and several hundred words have entered the language of various coastal groups.[6]

To believe that bark painting is somehow more 'pure' or 'authentic' than other forms of Aboriginal art is a naive, if hitherto, convenient belief. Most of the barks in public collections including early works collected in the 1930s, 40s and 50s were, in fact, produced for collectors. Whether these collectors were anthropologists or others sympathetic to the work as art, they were, in fact, interventionist and the work reflected this in various ways. An example of this can be seen in the first section of early acquisitions, which include bark designs produced on card in 1948 for collectors who found it more convenient to transport than bark. Urban art likewise is not a recent phenomenon. Since the time of European settlement, Aboriginal artists in towns and cities have been producing artefacts and other works for the European market. A work's intended sale does not preclude it being 'traditional' since the act of relating cultural truths is a means of renewing the traditions in an oral culture.

Continuity & Change

Aboriginal art has always been an expression of a complex religion and culture. In the ceremonial context, the act of painting about significant events defines and reaffirms the artist's cultural relationship with her/his land and ancestral past. Art is an integral part of a ritual life which encompasses a total world view. It is a process of renewal which connects the past with the present and provides a template for the future as well as unifying the earth, (above and below) with the universe. It connects the sequence of life and death with the patterns of nature ensuring a state of well-being. In short, it is part of the Dreaming, the crucible from which Aboriginal culture is sourced. The Dreamtime

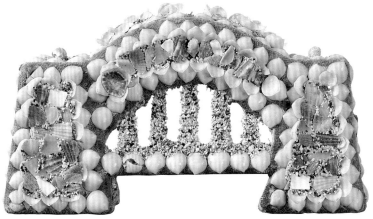

1

Artistic responses
to other cultures

Traditional bark painting techniques are employed to depict a Macassan prau (above) whilst dancers from Groote Eylandt and Numbulwar use flags to represent the sails in a ceremony (previous page). Similarly, artists living in urban areas adapted traditional materials and techniques in response to outside influences. This representation of the Sydney Harbour Bridge was made by an Aboriginal woman from the La Perouse community.

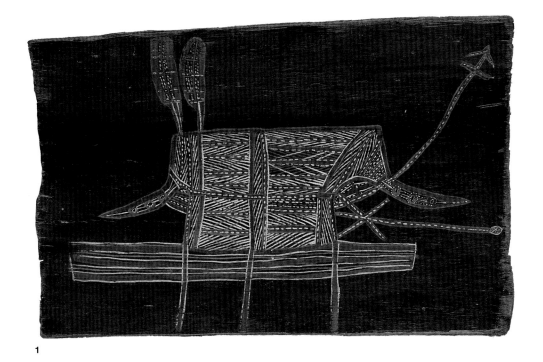

2

as it is often called, is a belief system that continually absorbs changes, which are in turn, revealed in new forms of cultural expression.

Before permanent white invasion, outside influences were varied, often transitory, though enriching as far as we know. However since 1788, European contact has been invasive and overpowering for many Aboriginal communities. Yet today, we see in the most affected regions, a cultural revival which has been mounting since the 1970s. Before that decade, the only Aboriginal artist known to most Australians was Albert Namatjira. The rise of an audience and market for 'desert art' in the late 1970s was paralleled by a renewed interest in bark paintings from Arnhem Land. This was followed in the mid 1980s by the emergence of 'urban' art shown in contemporary art spaces in the southern regions of the continent. The extraordinary richness and variety of Aboriginal art today reflects these rapid changes and also the exchanges between artists from different regions and diverse cultural backgrounds.

These changes and exchanges have, in turn, affected cultural frameworks, particularly for artists in towns and cities, who are finding new dimensions for their artistic expression. Aboriginal artists have enriched the bloodstream of Australian art and changed the texture of the contemporary art scene forever.[7]

The structure of this book

As already noted, the structure of this book deviates from the practice of organising Aboriginal art by geographic region. However, because The Art Gallery of New South Wales collection of Aboriginal and Torres Strait Islander art pre-dates the rise of art from the desert and from towns and cities as we know them today, it seemed appropriate to commence the tour with the theme, A Collection Begins, a section containing sandstone carvings and bark

paintings (or bark painting designs on paper). Similarly the final theme, Claiming a Space, – containing mostly 'urban' art with few barks – parallels collection practices and the diversification of art production over the past decade. Land Before Time, the second theme, refers to the period of creation, and shows works highlighting the epic creation cycles of the master painters of Arnhem Land produced in the 1950s, alongside new interpretations by artists from towns and cities 40 years later. Spirits of Place covers works dealing with spirit beings which inhabit the land and water – the earthbound variety, rather than ancestral beings. Apart from the ubiquitous mimi figures from West Arnhem Land, this section includes an installation of guardian spirits in papier-mâché in the 'urban' style. A very different depiction of the spiritual connection with land is revealed in the fourth theme, Land Maps. Ancestral journeys are mapped out across different terrains celebrating the Dreaming. Works range from a contour map of Groote Eylandt on bark, to eye-dazzling topographical canvases in acrylic from the desert, to a watercolour by Albert Namatjira. Within the new gallery, a number of these works will be mounted on floating plinths and viewed from above to emphasis effects of aerial perspective and the way they were painted on the ground. The idea of spiritual power invested in work by artists in the form of myriad dots, cross-hatching or other optical effects unites the wide range of works selected under the theme, Shimmer. Sorry Business, the fifth theme, is an expression used by Aboriginal communities around Australia for things associated with death. The works in this section reflect a human response to the mourning process and speak of the transitory nature of death rather than its finality.

Yanggarriny Wunungmurra
*Barama and Lany'tjung –
Yirritja Creation*
c1960
Plate 3

*The story of ancestral beings
Barama and Lany'tjung, although
belonging to the Yirritja moiety,
is associated with the great Dhuwa
creation stories of the Djang'kawu
and Wagilag Sisters .*

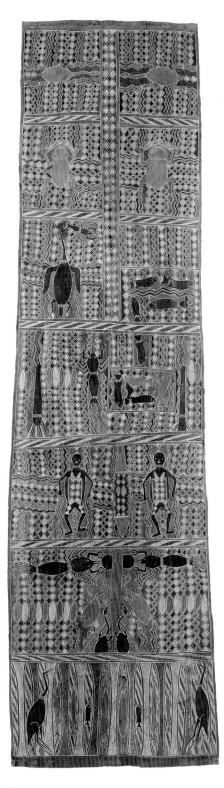

These seven themes are intended to introduce the reader to new ways of seeing a rich and complicated collection, but they also represent a personal view, formed in and amongst the constantly changing perceptions and projections of Aboriginal art in the 1990s. The process of responding to art from any culture involves individual perception, association and memory, which undoubtedly have played a part in the reading of the works contained in this publication. It has not been the author's intention to offend in any way.

The provision of a special place for restricted viewing of objects is one of the new directions to be taken by the Yiribana Gallery. It is an attempt to address the issue of the proper display of significant objects that are not totally restricted and need not be relegated permanently to the storerooms of institutions. It thereby makes an important point about the place of consultation with the communities from which these objects came. This display publicly recognises the continuing significance of these objects to Aboriginal and Torres Strait Islander communities and is a declaration of a partnership role in which communities retain ownership rights whilst the Gallery performs a guardianship role.

3

The Aboriginal and Torres Strait Islander Collection

The Art Gallery of New South Wales has long been recognised for the excellence of its collection of classical bark paintings. It is also regarded as a pioneer in the promotion of Aboriginal art, being the first state art gallery in Australia to actively establish a collection of Aboriginal art based on an enthusiasm for its aesthetic rather than its ethnographic qualities. The story of this collection is also the story of the growth of Aboriginal art in this country and the vagaries of collecting practices. Every piece bears witness to the complex background of changing perceptions, tastes and social attitudes against which both Aboriginal art and this collection have been developed. Like a living thread, the story connects the present with the past, reaching back to the curious origins of three small sandstone carvings from the 1940s, donated to the Gallery by well-known artist Margaret Preston in 1948. [1]

Wandjuk Marika translates artist Munggarrawuys story of a hunting scene to Tony Tuckson at Yirrkala 1959.

Two years later Tony Tuckson, who was then an attendant at The Art Gallery of New South Wales, saw a display of Aboriginal art from Arnhem Land at David Jones' Gallery in Sydney. Margaret Tuckson recalled his excitement when he returned home from the exhibition: "his fascination with the freedom of composition, and how he loved the way the artists allowed the shapes to flow over the edges when they didn't fit where they were meant to." As an artist himself, Tuckson felt profoundly moved by a sense of the spiritual which he saw in this 'primitive' work in much the same way Picasso and others had enriched their art with a study of African art in the early part of the century. Tuckson went on to become assistant to the Director of the Gallery in Oct 1950, from which position he would play a leading role in the development of the Gallery's Aboriginal art collection until his death in 1973 and in the conceptual relocation of Aboriginal art in the domain of Art.

In the late 1940s, [2] various scientific expeditions ventured to remote parts of the continent in the same spirit as an earlier generation of 'cultural explorers' who had penetrated 'darkest Africa' in search for knowledge. It was the gift to the Gallery of 24 barks and bark painting designs collected by the 1948 American-Australian Scientific Expedition to Arnhem Land (AASEAL) which really started the collection. All state galleries in Australia received similar gifts, but at The Art Gallery of New South Wales they produced dramatic effects. They were followed in the 1950s by intrepid individuals like Dr Stuart Scougall, an orthopaedic surgeon whose interest in bark painting had been kindled during several professional visits he made to Arnhem Land in the 1950s and Tony Tuckson, later to become Deputy Director of the Gallery. His and Tuckson's fascination with Aboriginal art led them on the first of several expeditions to the northern areas of Australia to collect works. Bark paintings were also, by this time, beginning to trickle down from Arnhem Land into southern galleries, where they were purchased by private collectors, including Scougall, at exhibitions of 'primitive' art across the country. [3] "It was only a matter of time before the art galleries in Australia began to form collections of Aboriginal art." And so it was – although for over a decade after his death, the Gallery's own collection seemed itself 'frozen in time'. [4]

The 1970s saw the emergence of Western Desert art in Central Australia. By the 80s the market for these works was beginning to take off in the southern cities. There was also renewed interest in bark painting which had undergone some changes and Aboriginal art was increasingly produced in non-traditional materials. Over this period, the Gallery relied on occasional gifts and purchases, acquiring few new pieces of Aboriginal art – though some of these would now be ranked amongst the most significant in the collection. In the 1990s, the emphasis in Aboriginal art is increasingly on the individual artist rather than the collective art of a regional group – and the works fetch contemporary art prices, rather than the fairly nominal sums paid for Aboriginal art works when they were traded as ethnographic artefacts. The Gallery is fortunate in, once again, having the ongoing support of patrons of Aboriginal art, the enlightened few who financed the purchase of key pieces of desert art and other works which now enable the collection to reflect the efflorescence in Aboriginal art over the past two decades.

However, the story of the collection really begins in 1956 when the Commonwealth Government gave the Gallery its first substantial intake of Aboriginal art as its share of the works collected by of the American-Australian Scientific Expedition to Arnhem Land (AASEAL). Jointly sponsored by National Geographic, the Smithsonian Institute and the Commonwealth Government, AASEAL was the first large-scale exploration into Arnhem Land, a region still little known to most white Australians. The 16 members of the expedition included medical, scientific and cultural experts, and 45 tons of gear! Anthropologist, Charles Mountford was the appointed art expert. After eight months camping at Groote Eylandt, Yirrkala and Oenpelli, (a proposed camp at Roper River was rained out), he had collected 400 to 500 paintings on bark and card (which he gave to the artists when bark was scarce or inconvenient to carry) along with numerous artefacts. [5] These became the property of the Commonwealth Government and in 1955/56 were distributed to all state art galleries across Australia.[6] A total of 10 barks and 14 works on paper came to this Gallery, then called the National Art Gallery of New South Wales. They included rare 'middle' period Groote Eylandt barks (delicate figures on velvet black manganese backgrounds) as well as drawings in crayon on card, and a number of Port Keats works

which were amongst the first works on bark by artists from that area. [7] Mountford helped pave the way for the appreciation of Aboriginal art for its aesthetic value by ensuring that the pieces were distributed amongst art galleries in preference to state museums, despite criticism from fellow anthropologists. At this time, the Australian art world was in the process of belatedly embracing modernism from overseas which incorporated elements of African and Oceanic art. The time was right for Aboriginal art to be seen by these audiences in terms of a new aesthetic.

The next expedition, nearly ten years later, was a pioneering feat of another kind. Dr Stuart Scougall, an avid collector and benefactor of the Gallery, accompanied by Tony Tuckson, and his wife Margaret and Dorothy Bennett, [8] Scougall's secretary, also headed north. Scougall was motivated by a sense of urgency based on 'salvage ethnography': like the missionaries and others of the period, he sincerely believed that the culture was dying. However, the specific purpose of the 1958 expedition was to collect [9] the most adventurous work of Aboriginal art that had ever been commissioned by a gallery. [10]

The 17 grave posts, known as the Pukumani Grave Posts have been a centrepiece of the Gallery ever since their installation in 1959. Tuckson's siting of the Grave Posts in the central forecourt publicly proclaimed that Aboriginal art was a 'living art form' more appropriate to art galleries than museums.

This installation was an awesome presence in its unaccustomed earthiness, scale and unfamiliarity to art audiences, and it had an immediate effect on a number of artists. Sali Herman, a Sydney artist, for example could not pack his bags fast enough to seek out the source of such inspirational work. [11]

This view, however was not shared by all. Douglas Stewart, wrote in the Bulletin on 1 July 1959: "... the graveposts... made a somewhat bizarre display... and most people, admitting that the poles are delightful in themselves, will wonder if the proper place for them is not the museum... though they have definite artistic merit of an elementary kind, are really in the nature of ethnological curiosities than works of art." In defence, artist James Gleeson wrote in The Sun newspaper on 18 July, 1959, "Whatever their symbolic significance might be they represent an ensemble of abstract shapes of aesthetic appeal". [12]

In 1959, the same group headed north to Yirrkala, a Christian mission in the Gulf of Carpentaria, and with similar prescience collected a series of major creation epics from the master bark painters of the area. These two expeditions led by Scougall, accompanied by Tuckson marked the beginning of serious collecting of Aboriginal art by the Gallery. [13] (see plates 11 and 13) In the same year the gallery purchased a small, but interesting group of bark paintings from Wallace Thornton – artist, teacher and a trustee of The Art Gallery of New South Wales – who had acquired them in Milingimbi over the previous ten years.

Dr Scougall, a strong-willed, energetic man who instigated and largely financed these expeditions, had been collecting independently across Arnhem Land, since the mid 1950s. As an orthopaedic surgeon, he had an abiding professional interest in why Aboriginal people stood on one leg. [14] This fascination first took him to what was then called 'Aborigine country' and whilst there, his interest in Aboriginal art was stimulated. He continued purchasing other pieces from the increasing number of exhibitions and auctions of Aboriginal art across the country. [15] Most of these he donated

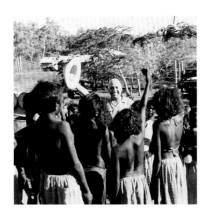

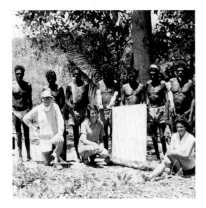

Top
Sydney artist Sali Herman raising his hat to reveal his bald head for the amusement of the children.

Bottom
The Expedition team: Tony Tuckson photographs Dr Stuart Scougall, Margaret Tuckson and Dorothy Bennett with the Yirrkala painters who were painting barks for The Art Gallery of New South Wales. Left to Right: Gunyulawuy, Mathaman, Munggarrawuy, Mutitjpuy, Wandjuk, Bunungu and Mawalan assembled under a cashew tree on the team's last day at Yirrkala in 1959.

to The Art Gallery of New South Wales in 1960 and 1961 and they make up much of the present day bark painting collection. They include monumental barks of complete myth cycles which he purchased in Yirrkala at the time Tuckson was commissioning for the Gallery. These historic works were done with impeccable detail because, at the time, the artists themselves feared that such stories might be lost with the impending mining operations in the area. Works of this period, style and subject matter known as the 'classical' period of Aboriginal art have been compared to the Renaissance period in Western European art. Another set of works on complementary religious themes, albeit less epic, was purchased by the Gallery in 1962 from the Reverend Edgar Wells, supervisor of the Methodist Mission at Milingimbi from 1949 to 1959. Included in these 158 works were some 50 sculptures of ceremonial significance referred to as 'totemic emblems'. Amongst the bark paintings were some very early works by Central Arnhem Land artist, David Malangi, one of whose designs appeared on the first Australian dollar bill when decimal currency was introduced in 1966 (see plate 38). The image was used on the dollar bill without his knowledge or consent, though he later received some recognition in an incident which anticipates contemporary campaigns aimed at safeguarding the copyright of Aboriginal artists.[16]

Then the tide went out on the Aboriginal art collecting activities at the Gallery. The great expedition era was over and soon Tuckson would no longer be there to drive things along with his passionate commitment. The Gallery's coffers were empty. All departments were feeling the pinch, and the Aboriginal area suffered from the lack of a curator to stake its claims. Instead a patchwork of consultants and staff from other departments 'kept an eye' on the collection. The 70s were for this Gallery, as for a number of others, a period of uncertainty of direction, but they were also times of consolidation after the feverish activities of the previous 15 years.

The Art Gallery of New South Wales was about to showcase for the first time, its entire collection of 'primitive' art from northern Australia. The exhibition was timed to coincide with the opening of the Sydney Opera House in 1973. This was the opportunity Tony Tuckson had been working towards for nearly 20 years and a fitting finale to his career. He lived just long enough to know it opened. The *Pukumani Grave Posts* once again took centre stage and as Margaret Tuckson recalls, they were "absolutely breathtaking, surrounded by a brown floor, walls and ceiling with spotlights. As people came down the marble staircase, rounded the corner and looked down upon them they would actually gasp".[17]

Meanwhile in the desert, a 'new' Aboriginal art form was flowering. By the early 1970s ceremonial sand and body designs were being transferred to wood panels and some years later to canvas by tribesmen living in a remote settlement in Central Australia. It is not surprising that this new art work was not being purchased at the time, quite apart from the Gallery's funding and staff difficulties. The institutionalised art world which had been fed on a rich bark tradition was unable to re-focus on this new work in acrylic paint on board. It was not seen as sufficiently 'authentic' for purchase.[18] It was just too foreign or not foreign enough for the 'primitive art' label under which Aboriginal art was still exhibited. These early works from Papunya, like the Hermannsburg School watercolours of a generation earlier were generally viewed by the white art world as transitional, 'impure' and only good for the tourist market.

How wrong they still were!

The Whitlam era (1972 to 1975) [19] brought many advances for Aboriginal people. With the appointment of art advisers to remote Aboriginal communities, art production escalated, servicing an expanding commercial and private market. Increased funding from a newly created Aboriginal Arts Board within the Australia Council encouraged new art forms and during the 1980s the board put its support behind emerging artists in urban and rural areas. The works of these artists were purchased not for the Aboriginal art collection, but by the Contemporary art department and the Prints and Drawings department. Dealing mostly with contemporary concerns, these works on paper looked and 'felt contemporary'. They included innovative prints and drawings from Jimmy Pike in the Great Sandy Desert, Sally Morgan, urban artist from Western Australia, Kevin Gilbert political activist, poet and artist, Robert Campbell Jr, and Raymond Meeks from New South Wales.

The groundwork for these purchases had been laid by Bernice Murphy, curator of Contemporary art from November 1979 to December 1984, and the instigator of the first Australian Perspecta exhibition of contemporary art in 1981 at The Art Gallery of New South Wales. When the doors opened to the show, there was an air of discomfort. Exhibited beside the confronting conceptual installations that were synonymous with contemporary art at the time, beamed three huge 'museum pieces' of strongly coloured, extraordinarily detailed and meticulously executed acrylic paintings by the artists of Papunya Tula. [20] It was the first time most people would have seen desert art on a wall, let alone in this context. "It was an incredibly courageous thing to do at that time when the art world still viewed Aboriginal art in general as utilitarian, naive and unreflexive." [21] The relationship between desert designs in sand and synthetic polymer on canvas was a conceptual

leap few people could make, and the exhibits were viewed with some suspicion, as was desert art in general. [22] Murphy was shocked to find that people she least expected to be perturbed believed that there was some kind of 'sacred divide' between black and white Australian art. Aboriginal art belonged 'somewhere else' not in a survey of contemporary Australian art. Murphy believed that Aboriginal 'ground paintings' in acrylic on canvas had been excluded from art museums because of quite artificial strictures placed around the question of their 'cultural authenticity'. [23] With her help, the door was now firmly opened to this form of contemporary Aboriginal art.

In the intervening decades, the bark painting tradition had absorbed new influences and the Gallery continued to build, albeit slowly, upon its now comprehensive collection of work. Djon Mundine, the art adviser from Ramingining was appointed in 1984 as the Gallery's Curator-in-the-Field, the first time an Aboriginal person had been appointed to a curatorial position in an Aboriginal art department of a public gallery. [24] Mundine acquired a series of barks by David Malangi [25] on the topical issue of land rights which connected to the earlier controversy about his work, and some works by Dorothy Djukulul, one of the few female bark painters from Central Arnhem Land. Lino prints from Yirrkala about the great creative cycles purchased from Mawalan's daughter, Banduk Marika, also complemented Mawalan's epic sagas on the same theme collected by Tony Tuckson 30 years earlier. Together these works demonstrate the degree of artistic innovation that has occurred within a traditional context: from male to female, from monumental barks to small linocuts on paper in new designs. During this period, barks from the 1950s were donated by Margaret Tuckson and a significant gift of 38 bark paintings mainly from Central Arnhem Land

collected in the 1970s was received from physicist, Professor Harry Messel.

In 1988, The Art Gallery of New South Wales reopened its expanded, redesigned and rehung Aboriginal and Melanesian art sections. It was, at the time, one of the largest concentrated displays in Australia with over 200 paintings and some 50 other pieces of sculpture, jewellery and weaponry. However, it showcased a collection which had not taken up the lead given by Bernice Murphy seven years earlier, making it difficult to meet expectations that this exhibition would put a distance between the ethnographic shows of earlier years and relocate Aboriginal art, for the viewing public, as a vital and distinctive contemporary art form.

Serious gaps in the collection remained. The purchase in the 1990s of some spectacular key pieces of desert art produced between 1976 and 1988 has filled some, but there is no doubt that this Gallery, like others, missed out on the early Papunya works on board, just as it did in the 1940s and 1950s with early paintings by Namatjira and others from the Hermannsburg school. These, of course, are now offered by private collectors at the high prices in a market eager for works of historical value. Filling the gaps in any collection is always an expensive exercise, even if there are sometimes advantages in the 'wait and see' approach which the Gallery effectively adopted towards new areas of Aboriginal art production.

The impact of Aboriginal art on the contemporary art scene is reflected in a number of ways in the Gallery. The Aboriginal collection came under the umbrella of the Australian art department in 1990. This relocation signaled a change of attitude in which Aboriginal art is no longer marginalised, but allowed to be seen as an integral part of the Australian art scene – it is, after all, the work of the original Australians. The purchase of works from Aboriginal artists by departments other than the

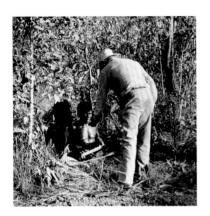

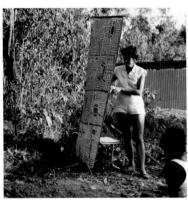

The top picture depicts Tony Tuckson recording the artists' stories about the bark painting being held by Dorothy Bennett seen below at Yirrkala in 1959.

Aboriginal art department (Contemporary, Photography and the Prints and Drawing departments of the Gallery), sends the same message. Large single-focus exhibitions such as the Aboriginal Women's Exhibition, 1991 (curated by Hetti Perkins and mounted in collaboration with the Contemporary Art department) and My Story, My Country, 1992 (with the Public Programmes department and curated by Ursula Prunster and Hetti Perkins) also demonstrate the Gallery's responsiveness to contemporary issues in Aboriginal art, and its cultural significance for the artists.

The way forward looks promising with renewed purchasing power and the appointment of a full-time Aboriginal curator. In 1994 Daphne Wallace was appointed permanent head of the Gallery's Aboriginal art department, becoming the first Aboriginal curator to occupy such a position in an Australian public art gallery. The Aboriginal art department is the recipient of an acquisition fund created by Mollie Gowing in 1992. Emily Kngwarreye's superb painting from Utopia was the first purchase from this fund, followed by Possum Love Story 1986 by Michael Jagamara Nelson and other works of significance, totalling 14 to date. This purchasing fund is currently being used to keep the Gallery's collection abreast of developments in Aboriginal art from towns and cities.

The current focus on boosting the collection with works from artists in New South Wales reflects the Gallery's commitment to this state as one of the most active art producing regions.

Works from the east Kimberley region, including some commissioned ilmas, have recently been balanced with a gift of 40 carved sandstone heads from the west Kimberley. An ilma is an all-embracing term for ceremonies and the string cross constructions used in them to tell stories passed on to living heirs by the spirits of departed people. The artist, Roy Wiggan of the Bardi people from Sunday Island, near Broome, Western Australia, received stories from his recently-deceased father which are embodied in the constructions.

The re-siting of the Pukumani Grave Posts, commissioned in 1958, to the sculpture garden in the new space heralds a new era for Aboriginal art at the Gallery. The posts have become historic markers, silent witnesses to the progression of the Aboriginal and Torres Strait Islander collection and a tribute to the late Tony Tuckson, and all those who followed. [26]

Margo Neale
Curator

There are many kinds of Aboriginal art, and therefore many different approaches to it. Aboriginal artistic achievements (like Aboriginal people themselves) form a continuum of many shades of difference – extending from the remotest outback to the heart of the big city; from a world bound by sacred lore to a world marked by personal ambition and political struggle; from the traditional practices of the world's most ancient continuous culture to futuristic explorations of high-technology and the information super-highway.

However, until relatively recently, there was considered to be an unbridgeable gulf between traditional and non-traditional art. It was assumed that one was authentic and the other inauthentic. Traditional art was pure and thoroughbred – almost beyond criticism; while urban art was tragically muddled and adulterated – and it could be criticised as harshly and intolerantly as you liked.

During the 1980s, there was a vigorous and successful campaign to redress this prejudice. In the 1990s traditional and urban art have been placed on a more equal footing, but does that mean that both are now beyond question? Are both to be judged by completely different criteria from the way we look at non-Aboriginal art? And if so, are a viewer's responses (liking or disliking, understanding or not understanding) irrelevant?

Is it necessary to restrain our imaginative engagement and deny our enjoyment of Aboriginal art because we are self-conscious about its difference? Or does the over-estimation of difference result in such an inhibition and poverty of comment on the one hand, and such indiscriminate reverence on the other, that both can inadvertently give the very negative impression of critical indifference?

These questions cannot easily be answered, nor can they easily be dismissed. However, there can be no doubt that a viewer's open-minded receptiveness and pleasurable appreciation would be welcomed by each and every artist. Aboriginal people are responsive to aesthetic qualities and are considerate of the formal beauty of their works. They too, realise that some artists are more able, more sensitive and ingenious in their use of materials and imagery than others – so, to admire the beauty and skill of a work would be an entirely appropriate response.

Aboriginal artists in this day and age are aware that their work is made for exhibition to strangers, that it is for sale, is collected by museums and will be preserved for posterity. In this sense, they are fully aware that what they are producing is Art. Nonetheless, it is important to realise that there has been a process of adaptation and reconciliation to European notions of Art.

In western societies, people generally assume that art is independent of most other aspects of culture, but this assumption is quite alien to Aboriginal tradition. Similarly, Aboriginal tradition gives little consideration to factors of self-expression in a work of art – a bark painting would not be regarded as a unique, essentially private view of the world, for example.

It seems a paradox that the many byways of Aboriginal art lead us into a multitude of difficulties and differences, because the very inclusiveness of the concept of 'Aboriginal art' also encourages us to look for unity in diversity. For Aboriginal people, art has provided a means of bringing different worlds together. It has played a dynamic, constantly evolving role, enabling people to communicate the things that matter to them – to one another, to Australians generally and onwards to the world at large. Through the high quality of their artistic achievements, Aboriginal people have gained attention, respect, understanding, and won an honoured place in the mainstream of Australian cultural life. This is an accomplishment that anyone can celebrate.

Terence Maloon
Public Programmes, AGNSW

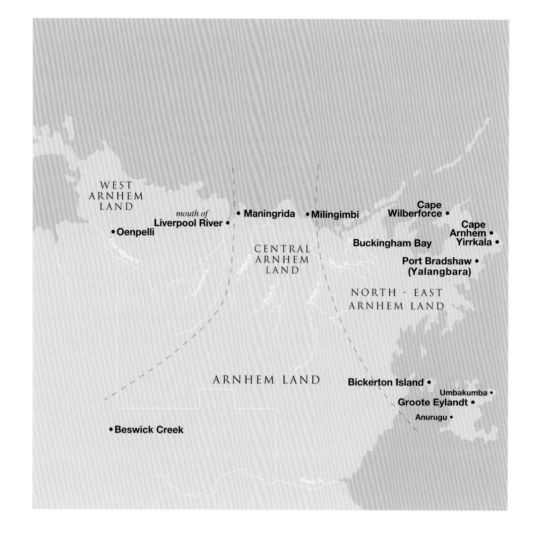

WEST
ARNHEM
LAND

mouth of
Liverpool River •   • **Maningrida**   • **Milingimbi**

• **Oenpelli**

CENTRAL
ARNHEM
LAND

Cape
Wilberforce •

Cape
Arnhem •
Yirrkala •

Buckingham Bay

Port Bradshaw •
(Yalangbara)

NORTH - EAST
ARNHEM LAND

ARNHEM LAND   **Bickerton Island** •

Umbakumba •

Groote Eylandt •

Anurugu •

• **Beswick Creek**

A COLLECTION BEGINS

This selection of works, mostly on bark and card from the late 1940s, takes the viewer back to the beginnings of this now impressive collection. It serves as a point of reference from which to assess its evolution. From these works, we can also judge the development of Aboriginal art in terms of how it has been made, collected and exhibited over the last four and a half decades. The eight paintings and drawings that follow are from the 1948 American-Australian Scientific Expedition to Arnhem Land (AASEAL). Painting on bark for an 'outside' audience was then a relatively new phenomenon and these were among the first images on bark to be widely seen. They are small and portable, reflecting in both size and style the manner and the times in which they were collected.

In a sense these works 'happened' to the Gallery when it became a recipient of a gift of 24 works in 1956 from the AASEAL expedition. The 'cultural explorers' who ventured to the remote northern parts of the Australian continent to collect them were looking for works of artistic merit – a reversal of Pre-War collecting practices in which Aboriginal art work was valued primarily as ethnographic documentation. Charles Mountford who was the art specialist with the expedition collected some 500 paintings and drawings on bark and paper as well as hundreds of other artefacts, which became the property of the Commonwealth Government and were subsequently distributed to state galleries.

The AASEAL expedition was the first major scientific collaborative project between Australia and the United States. Its 16 members, including scientists, a film-maker and a journalist carried out their studies at 3 different camp-sites across Arnhem Land over 8 months in 1948. The following works trace, in part, the expeditions movements.

In these bark paintings simple, single motifs of everyday subjects have replaced the complex images – often of a secret, sacred nature – seen in rock art in these areas. Irregularly shaped, they show little concern for the refinement and 'polish' which was demanded by emerging commercial markets from the late 1970s. They are figurative with a rawness and charm very different from the more ordered rectilinear bark paintings collected in the region, particularly from Yirrkala, in the 1950s. Unlike the children's drawings to which they have been compared, they are not grounded to a baseline, but appear to float like images seen in the art of Paul Klee and Joan Miró, and despite their apparent simplicity, they function on many levels. Some are records of everyday events and others function as visual cues to a complex repertoire of rituals associated with sites or events of significance.

Of particular interest in this section are the two sandstone carvings by Nora Nathan and Linda Craigie from northwest Queensland. These were donated in 1948 by Margaret Preston, a well-known artist who was one of the first to see artistic merit in Aboriginal art, and published her views in Art in Australia in December 1927. [1] Her interest was limited to the use of pattern and design and not their cultural meaning. The production of these works pre-date those from the AASEAL expedition. They are also works by Aboriginal women artists, which did not appear again in the Collection until Dorothy Djukulul's bark painting, Warrnyu – Flying Fox was purchased in 1985. The significance of this gift by a woman artist at that time can only be fully appreciated from the perspective of the 1990s.

Nora Nathan
Emu Egg Hunting

Linda Craigie
Two Ladies Waiting

Right top
Linda Craigie
Two Ladies Waiting
c1940
Plate 4

Right bottom
Nora Nathan
Emu Egg Hunting
c1940
Plate 5

Emu Egg Hunting
The hunting party consists of two or more people and a dog. The male emu sits on the eggs because he is the more aggressive. When the emu hears people approaching, he becomes stiff like a stick. In order to obtain the eggs, one person acts as a decoy and draws the emu from its nest. The emu also chases the barking dogs. When Aboriginal people take emu eggs, they leave up to three eggs in the nest so that the emu will lay there the following year.
Story from Daphne Wallace

These figurines in light-coloured sandstone from Djarra, southwest of Cloncurry in northwest Queensland, were presented to the Gallery in 1948 by Margaret Preston. Preston, an Australian artist renowned for her use of Aboriginal influenced motifs in her work and her advocacy of the aesthetic qualities of Aboriginal art,[2] collected these pieces on one of her trips north. Chiselled in flat planes, they have a "naive almost Gothic simplicity"[3] – qualities that would have appealed to Preston's preference for planar and incised designs, evident in her own lino prints.

They are reminiscent of the universal image of the earth mother or fertility goddess, with Asiatic, or perhaps, Islander features. Little is known about the background of these works, but sandstone figurines of this type were rare, according to current knowledge. It is possible that they reflect influences from cultures – known to have visited northern coasts in earlier times – which spread to inland areas. The works are similar to sandstone carvings which were being done on the Torres Strait Islands for a short period in the early 1900s. Carvings in wood on Melville Island, to the west, also bear a strong resemblance to these figures. The importance of the earth mother generative principle and its relationship to land is a common theme throughout Aboriginal culture and has a strong focus in the works dealing with the Djang'kawu and Wagilag Sisters' cycles that follow under the theme *Land Before Time.*

Nora Nathan – related to Linda Craigie – describes the progress of a hunt in *Emu Egg Hunting*. The hunters are two women, one of whom carries a coolamon (a wooden carrying dish) to collect the eggs. The other has a stone which she will use to drive the emu from his nest if the dogs do not succeed. The large bird, although it appears unperturbed, is rigid and poised for battle.

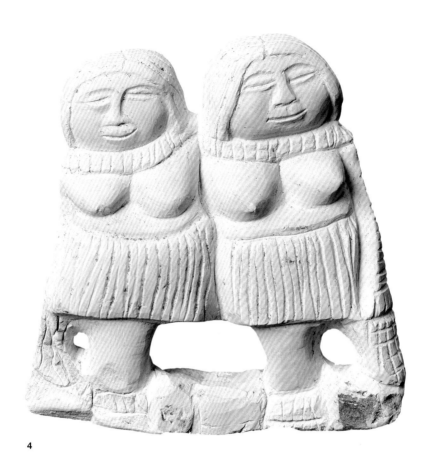

4

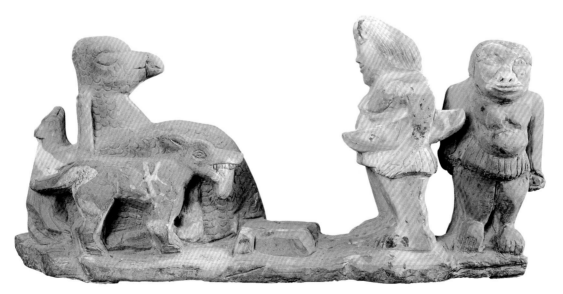

5

Expedition camps

Manggangina Wurramara
The Kestrel
1948
Plate 6

The anthropologist Charles Mountford documented the works he collected in 1948 and his notes form the basis for the following description. The Gallery acquired the pieces in 1956.

Expedition camp 1: Groote Eylandt

Groote Eylandt is located in the Gulf of Carpentaria, some 50 kilometres from the coast of North East Arnhem Land and 630 kilometres east of Darwin. The largest of an archipelago that includes Chasm and Bickerton Islands, it is 2,300 square kilometres in size. Because of its magnitude those living on the smaller island nearby have always called Groote Eylandt 'Ayangkwulyumuda', meaning 'big island', which is also the name used to describe the Australian mainland. Its close proximity to the mainland means that the people of Groote have similar belief systems, but they have developed a distinctive pictorial style closely related to a rich rock art tradition and their sea-faring lifestyle.

The two bark paintings entitled Dugong Hunt by Jabarrgwa (Kneepad) Wurrabadalumba and The Kestrel attributed to Manggangina Wurramara and a third Scrub Fowl (not pictured) attributed to Numayaga Wurramara, were painted in 1948. They reflect the importance of the sea to the livelihood and culture of the Groote Eylandters. All these creatures are important totems, marking out clan lands and the subject of ceremonial activities. The kestrel camped with his wife and children at a totemic place on the shores of Uralili Bay, western Bickerton Island. At that time, he was a man and every day he went out hunting, bringing back all kinds of food which he cooked at his camp fire. When the kestrel and his family left their camp at Uralili Bay, they were transformed into birds; their camp became a hole at

the top of a cliff and their camp fire a series of markings and water stains on the high, eroded cliff nearby. From Uralili Bay the kestrel and his wife went to Ilja-pilja-madja, where they dug a hole, made a nest and hatched out a family of chicks. The nest is now a waterhole in the middle of a large depression. The kestrels then travelled to Moanda-madja, on the west coast of Port Langdon on Groote Eylandt, where they rested before continuing their journey southwards. (Today their camp is one of three low caves, made by the erosion of the sea cliff.) Finally, they journeyed down the east coast of Groote Eylandt to Mangala. At Mangala there are three caves where, it is believed, the kestrels still live.

The bird in Scrub Fowl is similarly shaped to the kestrel, and this is typical of the way all birds are depicted on Groote: small heads, small feet and bloated bodies. The kestrel is differentiated from the scrub fowl by the tail shape and the addition of wings. Charles Mountford noticed:

"... that in all Groote Eylandt paintings the birds were shown with short legs, I asked one of the men to make a picture of the brolga, a particularly long-legged wading bird (the outcome) of that request indicates that all birds are drawn to a more or less traditional design, there being little attempt to make the paintings true to life. There is, for instance, but slight difference between the length of the legs of the brolga and those of the kestrel."

Dugong Hunt depicts a successful dugong hunt in action: the harpoon rope swings through the air, the spearhead finds its mark and the fisherman with arms raised thrusts the harpoon home. The man in the middle manning the oars, which are seen projecting below the boat, is of less importance to this moment of capture and is pictured smaller than the harpoonist. The third man at the rear skillfully keeps the substantial dugout canoe on course.

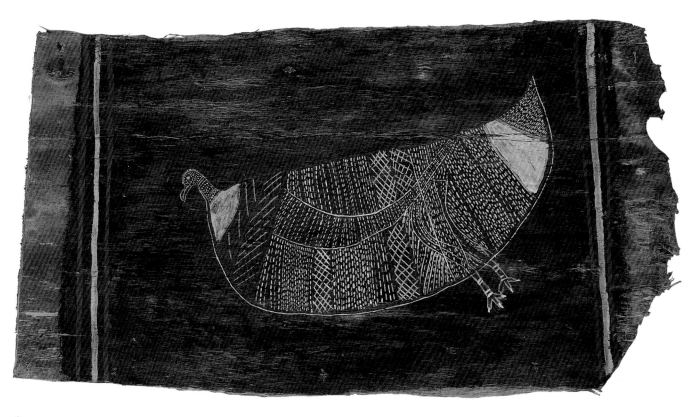

6

Right top
Artist unknown
*Bayini, men and women
of Port Bradshaw*
1948
Plate 7

Right below
**Jabarrgwa (Kneepad)
Wurrabadalumba**
Dugong Hunt
1948
Plate 8

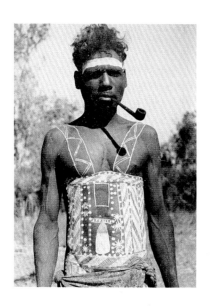

*A complex design
appears on the body of
an older ceremonial
person in accordance
with his ritual status.*
Photo c1960 courtesy of
Angus and Robertson

The dugong, a mammal commonly referred to as a 'sea-cow' is prized for its flesh. It is also the subject of important ceremonies. The dugong spirit is believed to have come from the mouth of the Roper River on the mainland and travelled northward along the coast and crossed over to the western side of Winchelsea Island where it made a freshwater spring. From there it dug down through the earth and travelled underground to the eastern shore of the Island. This spot is visible today as a depression in the sand and is an important ritual site for ceremonies to ensure the continuation of the dugong.

The style

These works, although done with natural ochre paint, bear a greater resemblance to drawing than painting. They have a free flowing linear quality. The outlined shapes silhouetted against a dark background seem to float in space. The black pigment used on Groote Eylandt comes from manganese found on the island whereas charcoal was used in other parts of Arnhem Land. Today some artists prefer to use the stronger black from burnt rubber tyres – of which there is no shortage if you can stand the smell. Lines, cross-hatched, broken and dotted, fill the inside of the shapes in an intricate patterned web. Like tiny visual fields of energy, these colourful dots and dashes shimmer.

The similarity of these simple images on plain backgrounds to the art of West Arnhem Land is not surprising, as both areas are linked by their rich rock art traditions. However, the use of a black background on these barks is not only unique to Groote Eylandt, but also to a particular period in the 1940s and 50s. The influx of miners in the 1960s created a new market which preferred more complex compositions and overall patterning.

Expedition Camp 2
Yirrkala

After 14 weeks on Groote Eylandt the expedition moved to Yirrkala, a coastal mission on the mainland north of Groote. Charles Mountford started giving card to the artists because it was lighter and more portable than sheets of bark – an important consideration given that they were already carrying 45 tons of gear in difficult conditions. Bark was also scarce during the dry season. For similar reasons of convenience and availability, some four decades later artists throughout Arnhem Land are experimenting with traditional designs on paper.

Bayini, men and women of Port Bradshaw is painted with natural pigment on green paper. The Bayini are described by Mountford as a "puzzling fair-skinned people who during early times went to Port Bradshaw in search of trepang". The local Aboriginal people say they are a people who came just after the period of creation and before the Macassans started visiting. According to early writers, they may have been an isolated group of Dutch or Portuguese who visited the area at various times. Current writers believe they refer simultaneously to early Macassans and 'Wongarr Aborigines (creational beings)'. [4] Unlike the Macassans, the Wongarr brought their wives (and children) with them (represented by the two central figures) and carried long knives, pictured in the hands of the two outside male figures. They are painted with the wedge-shaped Yirritja cloud symbols which are repeated around the frame and are associated with Cape Wilberforce, Cape Arnhem and Port Bradshaw – the area from which the Milingimbi people originally came. It was suggested by anthropologists as early as the 1930s that the clan body designs from the Yirrkala area were developed by Aboriginal people from designs borrowed from early Asiatic visitors. Similar cloth designs of the cloud pattern are common in Central Celebes and in what was Dutch New Guinea.

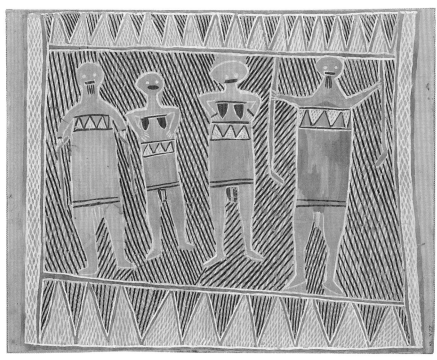

7

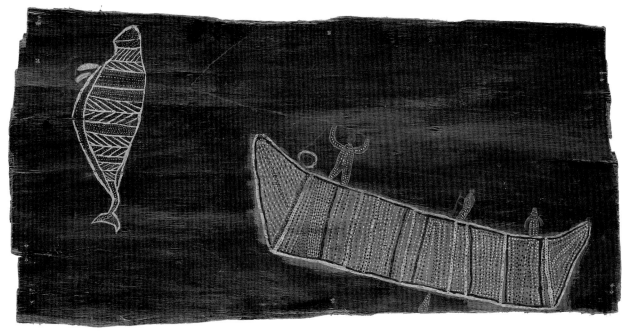

8

Right
Artist Unknown
*The Rainbow Serpent Narama
and her sons*
c1948
Plate 10

Below
Artist Unknown
The Wild Honey, Koko
1948
Plate 9

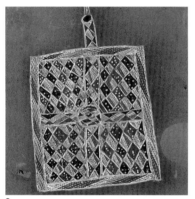

9

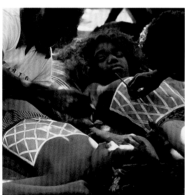

Above
*Young initiates are
being 'painted up' with the
'sugarbag' design for an
initiation ceremony which will
'make them into young men'.*
Photo Penny Tweedie Nangalala N.T. 1979

Expedition Camp 3: Oenpelli

Oenpelli was the expeditions last camp-site, 500 kilometres and eight months from their starting point. Today it is also known as Gunbalanya and is located approximately 50 kilometres inland near the East Alligator River. Stylistically, this painting is almost the inverse of the works from Groote Eylandt. The surface is completely painted over and the cross-hatching fills the space surrounding the figures, leaving the only blank sections inside the figures instead of outside. This overall patterning in sections remains a distinctive feature of art from Yirrkala, although the barks have become larger and more complex in response to the tastes of collectors and encouragement (in the past) of a 'craft' aesthetic by some art advisors. The Rainbow Serpent Narama and her sons, also on card, shows the female rainbow serpent and her sons in the sky. Narama usually lives among the rocks in the sea at the mouth of the Liverpool River, near present day Maningrida. She is highly coloured, with large ears and a beard, and has such a strong dislike of strange 'Aborigines' that should one of them approach her home she 'bites' their spirit and they die. When the serpent becomes annoyed she first makes a snuffling noise, then rises into the sky in the form of a rainbow creating clouds and rain.

Here she is depicted with her long ears and projecting tongue. Her sinuous body stretches from the lower right-hand corner of the painting to the upper left corner. Her sons form the diamond-shaped pattern around her, and the cross-hatched background represents rain clouds. The energy and power of this serpent when aroused is conveyed by the striking diagonals crossing in opposite directions; the rapid hatching in light over dark which curves with the forms and the larger-than-usual bold dots vibrating across the serpent's writhing bodies. The artist has captured the electrifying effect of stormy weather as well as the spiritual power of this being which belongs to the rainbow serpent family – the most powerful of all Aboriginal creative beings.

Milingimbi

The research team did not camp at Milingimbi although they did receive a small but valuable collection of barks from the mission superintendent Reverend Arthur Ellemor. These images revealed a similarity in design and mythological content with the art of Yirrkala, despite the vast distance by boat or foot between the two areas.

The Wild Honey, Koko is associated with the wild honey woman Birikura, whose camp was on the mainland south of Galiwinku (Elcho Island). This site is a totemic place of the wild honey, Koko. This conventionalised representation of a hive of wild bees is a design which is seen on bodies, poles, barks and canvas. The projection from the upper edge is the 'nose' or entrance to the hive and the central disc is the beeswax. The diamond shapes covering the painting, in-filled with cross-hatching, represent the honeycombs filled with honey. The white lines form the margins of the various cells and the beeswax, while the dotted diamonds are the eggs and young bees.

Honey which comes from the stingless bee, is one of the few naturally occurring sweet foods available to the people of the area. Many hours are spent searching for the hives and great shrieks of delight accompany a successful find. People come running from the bush in all directions for their share. They spend hours climbing trees and cutting out the hives – often referred to as 'sugarbags'. The honey stories are the subject of a complex repertoire of ceremonial activities.

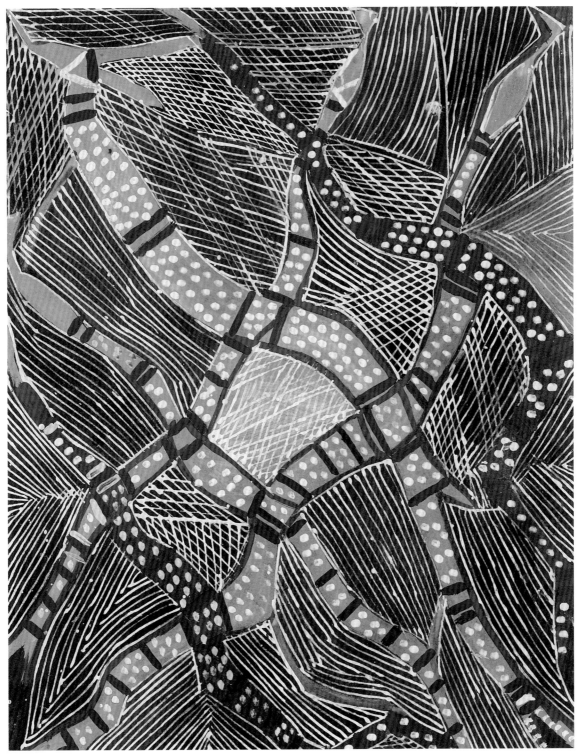

The Scougall Collection

The following three works from West Arnhem Land were collected by Dr Stuart Scougall who donated altogether 181 Aboriginal works to The Art Gallery of New South Wales. These were mostly collected around Oenpelli between 1956 and 1959 and also purchased by Dr Scougall from an exhibition entitled, Art from Arnhem Land at Qantas House, Sydney in 1961. They entered the Gallery's collection in the same year.

Spider Nabunu/Murulmirr
Long-necked tortoise c1956

The freshwater tortoise, which is the artist's totem, is prolific in the waterholes around Beswick Station near Katherine in the Northern Territory. The x-ray style is characteristic of the rock art tradition of West Arnhem Land and reveals the internal structure of the tortoise. A limited range of ochre colours has been placed on a plain background and the tortoise appears to be splayed, with the neck arched to fit into the available space. Surrounding the figure are some freshwater lobsters, also known as yabbies. The painter Spider Nabunu has a particular love of patterning, which is apparent in the combination of bold areas contrasting with the fine line work. The compression of the figure within the borders of the work is a device used widely in the area today, although on much larger works.

Jimmy Nakkurridjidjilmi
Mamalait, the starving children c1961

This intriguing line drawing on bark is a narrative about events that occurred at a place called Gudjamandji or Marra Falls. There are a number of variations of the story.

One interpretation tells of a family who camped close to Gudjamandji which is said to be inhabited by the rainbow serpent Ngalyod, who attacks the spirits of people who venture too near. The parents died and the children were left in the care of an old man who only fed them small amounts of nuts and fruit from the edible yam, seen growing (see plate 12). The children cried continuously from hunger. This annoyed the rainbow serpent, who rose from the bottom of the waterhole and drowned the children by flooding the countryside. Another variation tells of an older brother who returned from the hunt with his dog and a goanna. He shared the catch with his friends in a cave, but the younger brother rejected the food and cried endlessly for water lily roots, which are shown together with a tree that grows in rocky places. Two entrances to the cave and a small cave for the dog are depicted.

This work illustrates the pictorial devices of sequencing events in one frame and enlarging the most important character of the story which are common to many cultures.

Mangudji
Man who had leprosy 1961

Painting on bark not only recorded images of religious or ceremonial significance, but also expressed social concerns and events of every-day interest. Leprosy was an imported disease that ravaged the population in the early days of contact and left many people without limbs or, in this case, toes (see plate 13). The figure to the right represents a woman. It is possible that the spotting effect refers to the effects of disease.

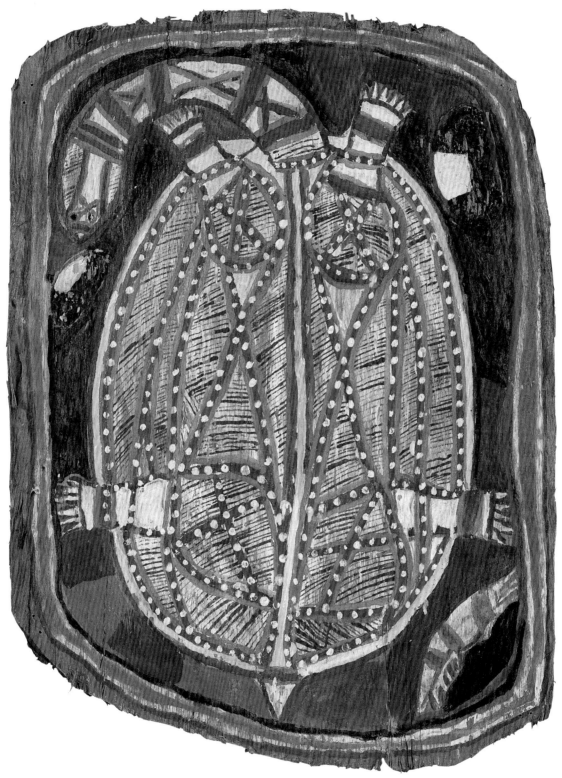

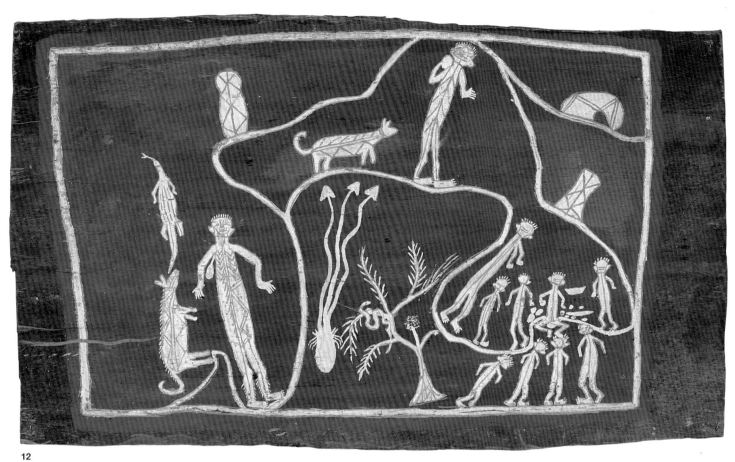

12

Above
Jimmy Nakkurridjidjilmi
Mamalait, the starving children
c1961
Plate 12

Right
Mangudji
Man who had leprosy
1961
Plate 13

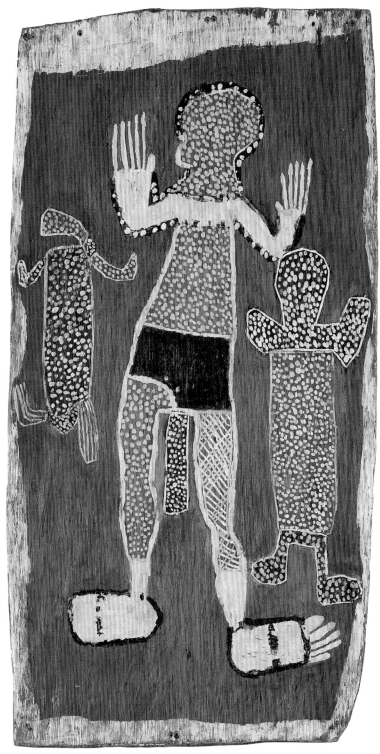

13

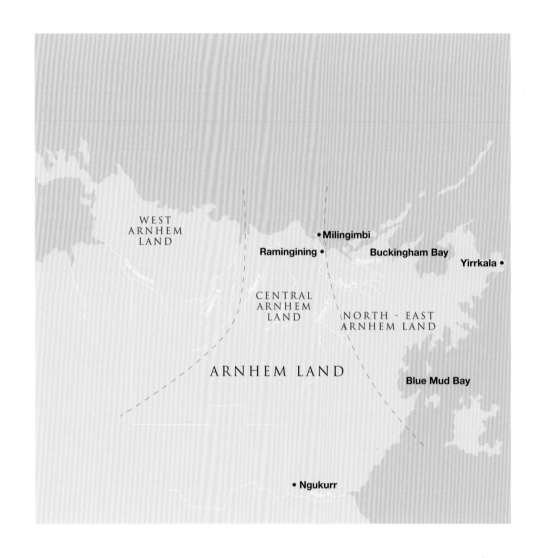

LAND BEFORE TIME

"At first there was nothing... The world had nothing on it, but it was not empty. Deep in the bowels lay coiled... the rainbow serpent... "[1]

The expression 'Land Before Time' refers to the period of creation. This section highlights not only the epic creation cycles of the master bark painters of Arnhem Land, but also new interpretations on canvas by artists from southern towns and cities. It is intended to reinforce the concept that although contemporary Aboriginal art is grounded in millennia of cultural continuity, it also involves interaction between European and Aboriginal cultures.

Creation stories in Aboriginal culture, as in a number of other cultures, generally tell of the migration of cultural heroes who are regarded as the ancestors of the group. These beings, who are not human (or only partly so), emerged from the ground at the beginning of creation and shaped the land as they journeyed across it. At the end of their travels, after they had taught men and women the techniques for survival and social rules, they sank back into the earth leaving their spiritual presence in water-holes and features of the landscape. Various events from their journeys are passed on in oral literature and visual records which still guide the social and religious lives of the people.

The two major creation cycles of Arnhem Land centre primarily on women in the universal tradition of the great fertility mother. The Djang'kawu Sisters travelled by canoe from an island to the north above the Gulf of Carpentaria, moving from east to west with the rays of the rising sun. In the East Arnhem Land version of the story, they are often accompanied by their brother.

They brought with them objects and symbols of their fertility – manifested in the perpetual pregnancy of the Sisters and the creation of waterholes. In the second and related cycle, the Wagilag Sisters travelled in a northerly direction overland, coming from southeast Arnhem Land, near present day Roper River (Ngukurr). In most recorded accounts, their activities were focused around Mirrarrmina waterhole in Central Arnhem Land where a giant serpent swallowed them and flooded the land. The rituals or episodes of this story emphasise the importance of the rhythmic cycles of nature, regeneration, rebirth and rules governing sexual behaviour. The Wagilag Sisters' story refers to people and events associated with freshwater, whilst the Djang'kawu Sisters' story refers to the saltwater people and their activities. Both creation cycles belong to the Dhuwa moiety and reflect Aboriginal people's dependence on their natural environment. Details of the stories vary according to regional interpretations, the degree of knowledge possessed by the artist and the part of the journey being referred to. The versions which follow are based on information supplied by Mawalan and Wandjuk Marika to Tony Tuckson and Dorothy Bennett. The quality of these narratives reflects their skill as storytellers.

In southeast Arnhem Land, Ginger Riley Munduwalawala's paintings depict another giant serpent, Bandian, who was involved in the creation of his mother's country, whilst Trevor Nickolls, an artist from Adelaide, places his guardian rainbow serpent in the Garden of Eden.

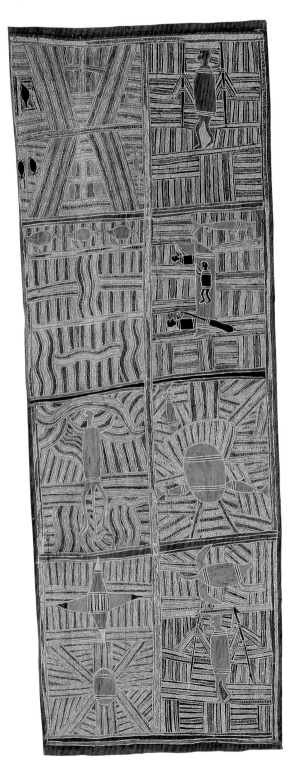

Left
**Mawalan Marika
Wandjuk Marika, Mathaman
Marika, Woreimo Marika**
Djang'kawu Myth (no. 1)
1959
Plate 14

Right
Mawalan Marika
*Ancestral Figure
of the Dhuwa moiety*
1959
Plate 15

14

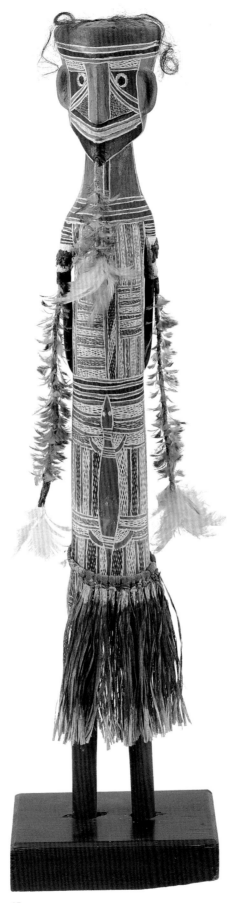

15

Mawalan Marika

Mawalan Marika was a master bark painter whose work in the early decades of this century coincided with the first stages of colonisation by Europeans in North East Arnhem Land. He has long been regarded as one of the true 'greats' of the bark tradition, a reputation he gained as a result of his vast knowledge, artistic inspiration and commitment to passing on his skills and knowledge to his children. He is reputed to be the first male bark painter to allow a woman, his daughter Bayngul, to paint important stories on bark.

Mawalan was a highly-respected ceremonial leader whose many early works were amongst the first significant body of barks collected by Tony Tuckson and Dr Stuart Scougall in the late 1950s. Mawalan and other ritual leaders were painting large collaborative works of the most important stories for collection, because the area was under threat from bauxite mining. Works with a scale and complexity, like this, have rarely been seen since that time. Dorothy Bennett, now a Darwin-based specialist on Aboriginal art, who was on the team, recalls how seriously the execution of these highly religious works was treated by the elders. The artists painted inside a circle, marked out on the ground, to ensure that neither women nor the uninitiated would get too close.

Mawalan, in collaboration with his sons and brother, painted this superb bark in 1959 at Yirrkala on the Gulf of Carpentaria (see plate 14). As a ritual leader and teacher, he designed and supervised the project – a process of preserving the culture through his sons. Each of the sons later became great painters of the Djang'kawu and related stories, as did his daughters. Many of their works have been collected by this Gallery.

This encyclopedic 8 panel bark depicts the journey of the Djang'kawu Sisters and their brother. It records their journey from Buralku, the Island of the Dead, to a place near Port Bradshaw called Blue Mud Bay on the east coast of Arnhem Land. In this region, the brother features as the most significant ancestral being in the cycle and although he dominates this bark, the cycle also refers to the trio. Together they made and named sacred animals, plants and places, allocated clan lands and instituted the rituals for the Dhuwa moiety.

Panel 1 (see diagram at left)
Right side, bottom corner

The brother is shown wearing a waistband of string decorated with parakeet feathers, a reference to the warm rays of the sun which accompanied their journey. He inserts his sacred stick or mawalan (also the leading artist's name) into the ground. Spring water gushes forth, bringing new life – an act which refers to the multiplication of the clans through the sexual act. Cicatrices of ritual scarring on his chest denote his ceremonial status. The horizontal banding indicates his footprints, while the gridding below his feet shows his camp on the Island of Buralku. Above his head, a brolga (a long-legged bird) on the clay pans is ready for flight. The various line patterns surrounding it refer to marks made when the brolga dances and digs in the ground for worms. The bird's feathers are shown with markings similar to the brother's. The khaki-green dividing line indicates the beach.

Panel 2
Right, second from the top

The Djang'kawu Sisters paddle their canoe, with the brother lying in the bottom, through rough seas shown as blocks of vertical stripes between the horizontal lines of the foam made by the paddle. A garfish is at the front, and lines from the canoe's stern suggest the wake.

This is a diagram of the Djang'kawu Myth (no. 1). (See plate 14)

Panel 3

Right side, third from the top

They sight a large sea creature, possibly a whale, shown with watermarks. The shape is also a reference to the sacred birth mats of the Sisters. The black lines projecting in a 'V' shape from the rear, represent the creature's tail and the radiating lines above it are the fringing of the mat, as well as the wake of the whale. The black dividing line refers to the deep sea.

Panel 4

Left side, third from the top

They see a thunder cloud, depicted as the Thunder Man. He is urinating, which forms a waterspout between cloud and sea and is itself the subject of many paintings. Weather patterns surround him, with an arching cloud above releasing rain.

Panel 5

Left side, bottom corner

As they approach the land, they look back and see the Morning Star – an important symbol for another set of related ceremonies (see plate 40) – which has guided them from Buralku. The brightness of the star is conveyed by the striped centre and the radiating lines. Later as they land at Yalangbara, Mawalan's country near Port Bradshaw, they look back and see the sun, Walu, rising amongst the rosy clouds shown as bands in the centre of the circle. The horizontal bands between are the rays of light which fall on various parts of Arnhem Land, reflecting off the water and the white sand.

Panel 6

Right side, top corner

The Djang'kawu brother at the landing place is surrounded by the sacred totems (rangga) brought from the Island of Buralku, which will bring life to the dry and lifeless land. The red and yellow ochres represent parakeet feathers which symbolise the rays of the sun and the

white is the foam of the sea. As they unload the canoe, the incoming tide (vertical lines) leaves marks on the beach (horizontal lines).

Panel 7

Left side, top corner

At a rocky place (diagonal lines) they hear the flying foxes in a sacred tree with nuts. They hear the black mangrove bird in its nest and the morning pigeon in the mangroves and see the lizard nearby. The oval shapes refer to the trepang or sea cucumber, also known as bêche de mer, considered a delicacy by the visiting Macassans and Japanese traders from the north.

Panel 8

Left side, second from top

At the water's edge, there are three whistling ducks; one male and a female with her chick. They leave a broken horizontal with diagonal banding behind them, as they swim. Waves breaking over sandbanks, in the shallows, are represented by wavy lines.

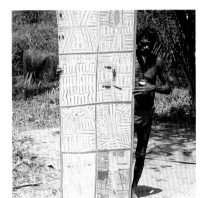

Mawalan holds the nearly completed bark painting of Djang'kawu Myth (no. 1).
Photo Yirrkala 1959

Mawalan Marika
Djang'kawu Creation Story

This bark painting, which is part of the Djang'kawu religious cycle, focuses on concepts of fertility associated with the creation of the clans. In the top panel, at the left, the Sisters are standing by a sacred waterhole with the overflow on each side seen as radiating lines. Another possible interpretation is that the circle is a swamp and the lines at each side are lily leaves. It has also been suggested that the red-ochred area, in which the Sisters appear to be lying, is a grave – a reference to Buralku, the Island of the Dead.

The brother is represented by a portrait of the artist (seen on the right hand side) sitting before his sacred goanna tail and singing:

Although I leave Buralku I am close to it,
I, Djang'kawu, am paddling
Paddling with all the paddles, with their flattened
tapering ends.
*Close I am coming with Bidjuwuraroiju.**
Coming from Buralku...
*[*one of the Djang'kawu Sisters]*

In panel two, below, the Djang'kawu Sisters are shown giving birth to the first people, the Dhuwa clans of the region, at a place not far from Milingimbi. The different colours refer simultaneously to the different clan groups and sexes – male children are yellow, female children are black. The Sisters populated the land as they moved over it, plunging their digging sticks into the ground to create waterholes which overflowed and fertilised the country.

The eight digging sticks, in the third panel to the left, grew into trees to create shade for the children. Four other yellow ochre rangga (important ceremonial objects) are shown as growing trees to the sides of these poles. In the adjoining panel, the brother is seen urinating, with the Sisters standing either side. The juxtaposition indicates his association with the Thunder Man, who is often depicted as a water spout. The two rectangular star shapes, on the right, refer to the Sisters' journey from the east on the rays of the morning star and then, to the west, travelling on the rays of the sinking sun. These designs are reminiscent of the 'Union Jack' but have always been a significant feature of this story and often appear alone as the subject of a painting (see plate 17). Before they were painted on bark, they were painted on bodies and on hollow log coffins and grave posts in funeral rites. They symbolise the spirit of the ancestors eternally regenerated in the clan and, in this context, they also refer to the pattern of the shifting sands on the beach at Yalangbara where the Djang'kawu first landed. Dhuwa artists typically use flag-like designs of rectangles filled in with parallel lines, while Yirritja artists use the linked diamond design specific to their clan.

The bottom panel is a symbolic repetition of the birth scene above. Female babies are placed under conical mats (shown one on either side of the Sisters) so that they are protected from the sun and remain fair-skinned. The mats contained the sacred emblems that are still used today to ensure continuation of the rites. Male babies are placed in the grass, (three smaller circles) so that as men they will grow beards and be strong.

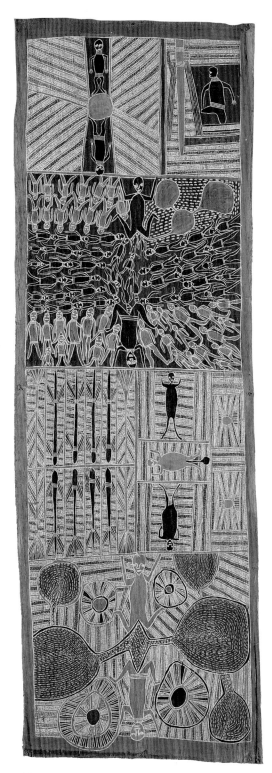

16

Micky Dorrng
Djang'kawu Sisters at Gariyak

Micky Dorrng
Djang'kawu Sisters at Gariyak
1994
Plate 17

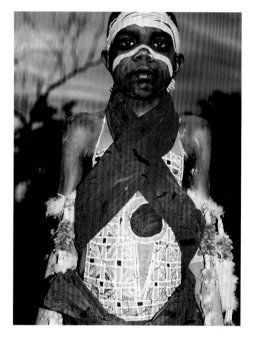

Bobby Bunungurr's son is painted for his initiation with a design which refers directly to the waterholes and other features of his father's country at Ngalyindi near Ramingining.
Photo Yaja 1993

Micky Dorrng of the Liyagawumirr language group is well known around Ramingining for his involvement in sacred ceremonies as an accomplished singer and performer. In the wider artistic community, he has a reputation for his boldly striped paintings and hollow log coffins representing the artist's land and 'Dreaming'.

This floor-piece, painted with acrylic on canvas, is based on ancient designs used in the Djang'kawu creation cycle and focuses on the Djang'kawu Sisters' activities in the artist's country. Viewing the work from above appears innovative in a gallery context, where one is more accustomed to works on the wall, but it reflects the traditional method of painting and viewing barks.

The whole Djang'kawu Sisters' story is often recognisable by this flag-like design, depicting waterholes created by the Sisters with their digging sticks in order to flood previously dry and barren land and encourage life. The radiating lines simultaneously refer to the rays of the rising sun and the Sisters' journey from the east. The same design can be seen in sections of much older bark paintings by Mawalan (see plates 14 and 16) on previous pages. The right to copy these designs is strictly controlled by a traditional ownership system similar to copyright, whether they appear on bodies, funerary poles, bark or canvas.

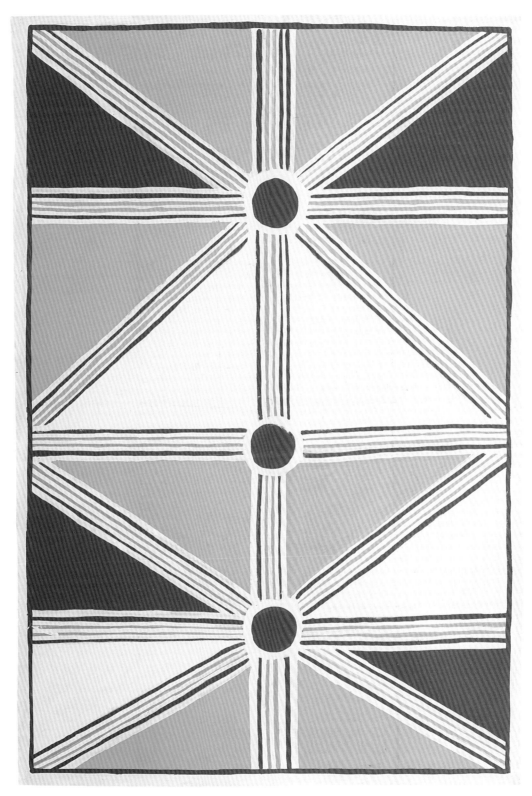

17

Dawidi Djulwarak
Wagilag Sisters' myth

Dawidi was a master painter and chief custodian of the Wagilag Sisters' story in the Milingimbi area of Central Arnhem Land. He inherited the Wagilag religious cycle in 1956 when he became leader of his clan group after the death of his uncle, Yilkarri Kitani.

The two Wagilag Sisters commenced their journey from the Roper River area, now Ngukurr, and walked north taking with them the baby son of the elder sister. During their long journey, they walked through long grass inhabited by stinging caterpillars, which are shown in a line alongside the Sisters' footprints in the bottom half of the painting (see plate 18). The younger sister gave birth to a child, and afterwards they decided to camp near a well (shown as a semi-circle at the bottom) in which the Great Python Wititj lived. The elder sister prepared a cooking fire. When the yams and animals they had collected were put on the fire, they came to life and ran into the well. A possum was chased by the elder sister's dog and ran into a hollow log (shown bottom right).

The younger sister's blood dripped into the well while she was collecting paper bark for a shelter. The smell of the blood so angered the Great Python that he sucked in the waters of the well and spat them out as clouds which rained and flooded the Sisters' camp. The Sisters danced, alternately beating the ground with yam sticks to keep the snake away and to stop the rain. Exhausted, they retired to their shelter. Wititj reared up, encircled their hut and swallowed them and their children. After a time, he regurgitated the Sisters onto an ant-bed and the ants bit them causing them to move. Realising they were not dead, Wititj seized a clapping stick and killed them. He swallowed them again, rose up into the sky, forming a rainbow, and fell

down to earth causing a loud noise like thunder. He left a triangular mark in the earth, shown with a black circle depicting the snake's heart and a white circle, his anus. This is the traditional shape of the ceremonial ground on which the Djunguan ritual is performed.

Other ancestral snakes questioned Wititj about the disturbance and what he had eaten. At first, he lied and then was forced to admit his error. He was made to realise that by swallowing those of the same moiety, he was breaking the law. He sickened, vomited out the women and retreated to his well, causing a strong wind. The rain stopped and the flood-waters that covered the land receded. Hearing the commotion, clansmen followed and found the Sisters' old camp and slept. In their dreams, the Sisters came to them and taught them the songs, dances and laws associated with this ancestral drama. They told them to go home and teach the people to ensure that the cycles of nature continued to fertilise the land.

The Wagilag cycle is the central focus of the Dhuwa moiety. Wititj the Great Python, sometimes seen as a rainbow, makes lightning with his tongue and thunder with his voice. The yellow bands at each end of the painting, indicate land and the cross-hatching depicts freshwater. This cycle belongs to the freshwater people, as opposed to the saltwater themes of the Djang'kawu cycle.

Dawidi's version of the narrative is more literal and detailed than earlier barks by his predecessor, Yilkarri. It is both a comprehensive and conventional representation of the story, belonging to what has been referred to as the 'classical' style. The degree of detail could only be undertaken by someone with the ritual status of Dawidi. It shows multiple representations of the Great Python in its male and female guises, as well as a possible reference to the two occasions

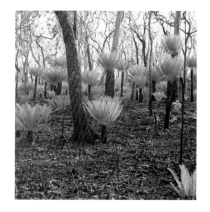

Cycad palms and other species are prolific in the sandy soils near Ramingining. The fan-shaped palm is a significant site marker and ceremonial emblem in the Wagilag and Djang'kawu Sisters' cycles.
Photo Yaja, Ramingining 1993

when it rises from the well. Not all artists of the Wagilag include such detail in their works, but instead refer to particular episodes from the cycle (see plate 19). There are many variations to the story depending on how much the artist wishes to divulge, in what terms and which part of the journey is being talked about. This account is based on that told by Dawidi to Dr Scougall at Milingimbi, 1960.

Dorothy Djukulul and Paddy Lilipiyana
The Wagilag Sisters' Story: Wurrutjurra – Sand Palm

Dorothy Djukulul was taught to paint important stories on bark by her father, Dawidi and her uncle Lilipiyana[2] from Central Arnhem Land. One of a small group of female bark painters, Dorothy Djukulul is arguably the best known and most accomplished, beginning her career in the 1960s after the death of her father. It is only since the 1960s that women have been given the rights to paint such important ceremonial cycles. Djukulul is a member of a socially and artistically prominent Ganalbingu family (her brother is George Milpurrurru). She now has the right to pass her knowledge on to both her sons and daughters. Lilipiyana was the chief custodian of the Wagilag religious cycle after his brother Dawidi died in 1970 and until his own death in 1993.

Both artists have rights to the Wagilag cycle through Dawidi. In this cryptic version of the story (see plate 19), the three semi-abstract verticals with the fan-shapes sprouting from each side are a reference to Mirrarrmina, the sacred waterhole where the Great Python swallowed the Sisters and regurgitated them, thereby instituting seasonal cycles and the laws of the land. In their abstraction, these stalks or trunks of the palm tree resemble the ceremonial rangga used to represent this event in ceremonies. It has also been suggested that these same shapes represent the digging sticks

the Wagilag Sisters used to hunt and to beat the ground in order to frighten off Wititj, the Great Python.

A comparison of this Wagilag painting with the previous one by Dawidi (see plate 18) reveals the enormous scope artists have in expressing a traditional theme. The silvery sheen produced by the thin white washes over dense black combined with the vibrant shimmering surface of myriad dots and fine cross-hatching (rarrk), evokes the spiritual power associated with this subject.

43

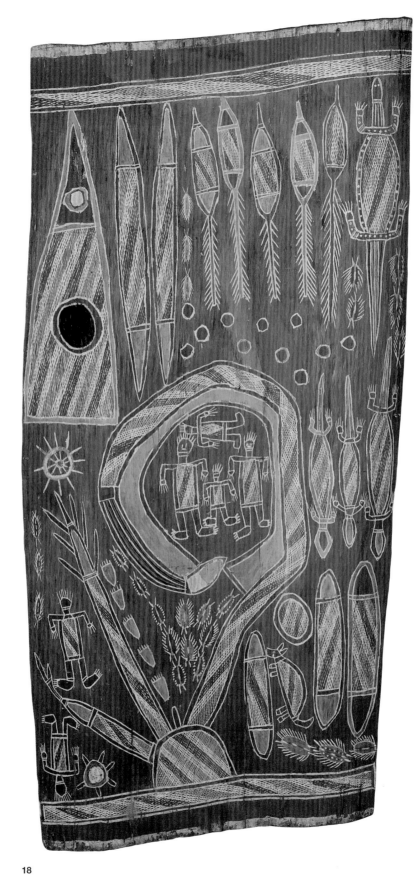

Left
Dawidi Djulwarak
Wagilag Sisters' myth
1960
Plate 18

Right
**Dorothy Djukulul and
Paddy Lilipiyana**
*The Wagilag Sisters' Story:
Wurrutjurra – Sand Palm*
1989
Plate 19

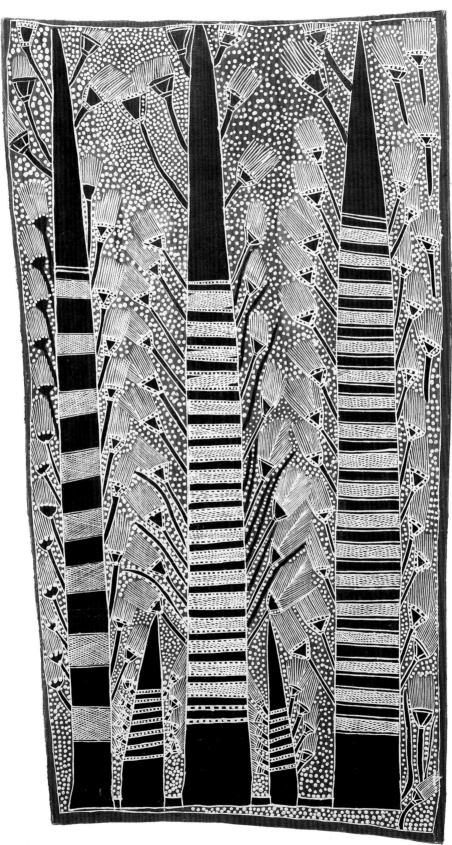

19

Trevor Nickolls
Garden of Eden

Trevor Nickolls
Garden of Eden
1982-84
Plate 20

"My painting is a marriage of Aboriginal culture and Western culture to form a style called... traditional contemporary – from Dreamtime to Machinetime... it is good to return to the Northern Territory and feel the spirit of the Dreamtime. It just knocks me out the moment I get into this country, it wraps itself around you..."[3]

Trevor Nickolls' work is motivated by the internal struggle he has experienced whilst finding his place as a person of mixed ancestry in what he calls an 'over-civilised world'. This conflict is often conveyed in images of alienation and aggression in an industrialised environment and contrasted, at other times, with themes of peacefulness and harmony in dream-like natural environments.

Garden of Eden, as the name implies, is a painting of harmony and balance. It was done between 1982 and 1984, during one of the more contented phases of Nickolls' life when he lived in Darwin and visited Aboriginal communities. It has been described as "an extraordinary blend of Byzantine and Aboriginal spiritual imagery"[4] and relates to both the past and the future. "It symbolises the innocence of man in Australia BC (before Cook) but also projects a utopian vision of racial harmony in the future."[5]

This is not only an allegorical painting but also, in a sense, autobiographical. Nickolls and his bride are painted living harmoniously in their landscape, he as a dusky Adam and she as a 'pellucidly pink Eve'.[6] The paintwork is detailed and dense, idiosyncratic as well as seductive. The lush greens, reds and blues carpet the canvas like an eastern tapestry, adding depth to an image of interracial love in the universal Garden.

A blue map of Australia painted with lapus lazuli brilliance, supplants the traditional location of a waterhole in the centre of a formal landscape. It functions like a mantle behind the artist and his wife, denoting a sense of ownership or belonging. Arrow-straight trees are arranged symmetrically around the central motif and their verticality is echoed by the lines of blue sky penetrating the land. The overall surface of the work is dense with dots and other markings found in desert art and bark painting, which flattens the landscape in a manner reminiscent of the thirteenth century Italian painter Duccio. Such influences are often reflected in Nickolls' work. Another influence is the Middle Eastern tradition of richly-decorated surfaces, studded with layers of intricate markings, as on Persian rugs.

Nickolls has maintained a fulltime professional career as an artist for 20 years. He came to prominence in the 1980s with an impressive body of work which was seen as bringing together two cultural streams: the old European – going back to pre-Christian days – and the ancient Aboriginal culture. Whilst elements from both sometimes harmonise in his work, mostly they erupt in visual ironies and contradictions that expose Nickolls' own search for identity between different worlds.

"Me being part black, part white, it's sort of like wrestling. I find myself in an attempt to keep my balance between the black and white."

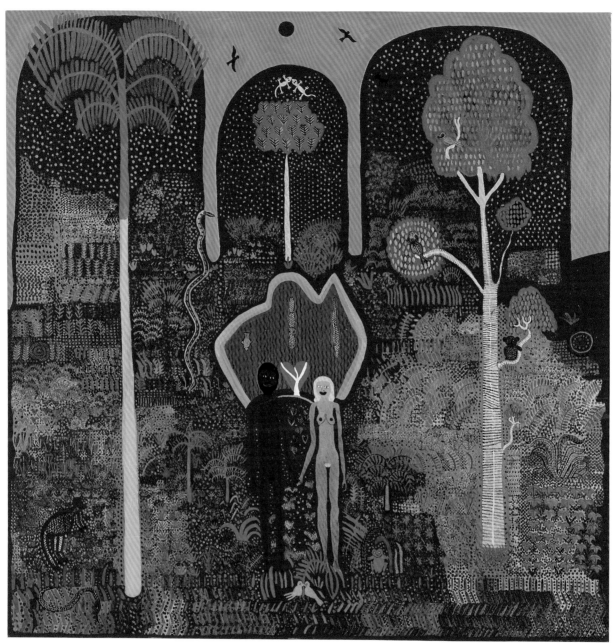

20

Ginger Riley Munduwalawala
Limmen Bight Country
1992
Plate 21

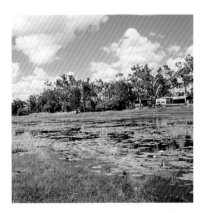

Top
*Ginger Riley Munduwalawala
surveying the Limmen Bight River.*

Bottom
*Ginger Riley Munduwalawala's
camp beside Marie Lagoon.*
Photos Beverly Knight, South East Arnhem Land 1993

Ginger Riley Munduwalawala
Limmen Bight Country

Ginger Riley Munduwalawala is a tribal elder who lives in his mother's country at Four Arches, 45 kilometres inland from Limmen Bight in the Gulf of Carpentaria. His virtuosity as a painter can be seen in the heroic scale of many of his paintings and by his individualistic translation of cultural traditions into new materials.

"In my mind I sit on a cloud on top of the world – and I want to paint what I look down on. That's in my mind."

Limmen Bight Country is the world Ginger Riley is looking down upon and the events he narrates are viewed in his 'mind's eye'. The painting is a visual narrative depicting the creation stories surrounding ancestral sites in the artist's country. It functions like a roll of honour to the ancestral beings responsible for the formation of the country. They appear in their various guises according to the different episodes in the story. Bandian, the great serpent who possesses many powers of transformation, appears as two fire-breathing snakes in the top panel, as benign guardian figures in the middle panel and captured in the beak of the sea eagle in the bottom register. Sometimes Bandian assumes the identity of the Rainbow Serpent, Wawula, or the fire-breathing sea-monster Bulukbun who kills people.

The work tells the story of the first being – the kangaroo shown in the bottom panel – who needed a mate to begin populating the earth. While travelling to a billabong near Ngalama, the kangaroo met Garimala the snake who told him to look for a young girl. This meeting took place by Ngamiyukandji – a rock near the confluence of the Limmen Bight and Cox Rivers that is of great significance to Munduwalawala. The spear wounds inflicted on the kangaroo

suggest that he has probably trespassed onto land belonging to another clan group.

The middle panel shows the Limmen Bight River and the geological formations created by the writhing motions of the giant serpent in two fire-breathing dragon-like manifestations, with their tails shown in the middle strip of blue. One female is guarding the eggs and their heads bracket the Four Arches in the centre top panel where they are creating a waterhole. A message stick announcing an important men's ceremony is guarded heraldically by two snakes called Garimala and Kurra Murra, who also protect the serpents' eggs in the roots of the sacred liver tree. Munduwalawala often paints message sticks which announce important men's ceremonies or issue an invitation to his country – which is symbolically enacted through viewing this work. The recurrence of Limmen Bight River as three blue bands dividing the panels reinforces its significance, as does the reference to the Four Arches in each panel.

The characteristic decorative red wedge shapes (forming the edge of the top panel) are derived from body designs, but were not otherwise explained. The omniscient sea eagle Ngak Ngak appears in the top panel – like a coat of arms – observing the creative dramas as they unfold in the tableaux below. The artist performs a similar guardianship role. Some have suggested that perhaps the artist bears witness through the eyes of his avian totem, but Ginger Riley sees Ngak Ngak as a separate entity. His identification with the events and with the Limmen Bight area reflects his belief that the creation of the first man, from whom he is descended, took place here.

Note: Ginger Riley, like a number of Aboriginal artists who are dealing with important stories, is subject to fluctuating sensitivities and politics within his cultural group. Therefore, since the time it was commissioned in 1992, this work may contain details that the artist may have subsequently chosen to withhold. The information, herein, has been compiled from a number of sources over time.

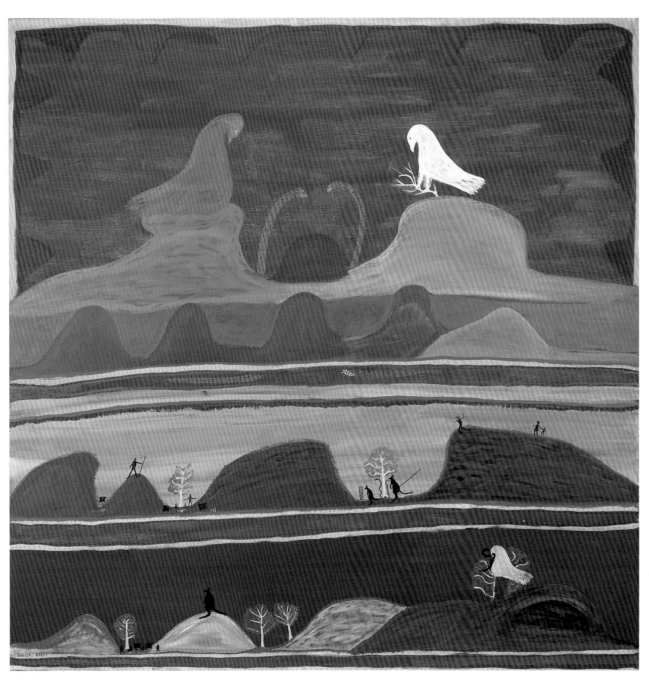

21

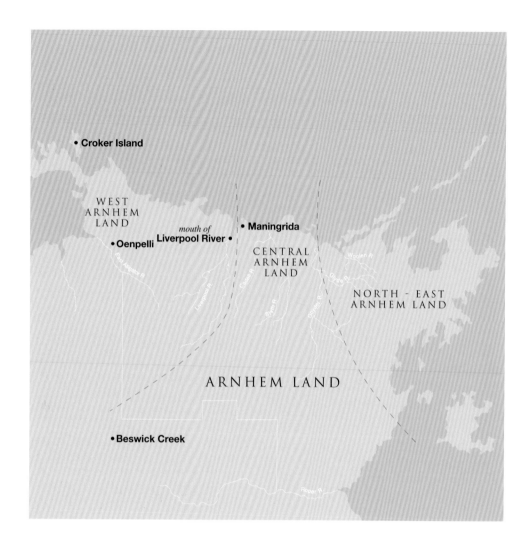

• Croker Island

WEST
ARNHEM
LAND

mouth of
Liverpool River •   • Maningrida

•Oenpelli

CENTRAL
ARNHEM
LAND

NORTH - EAST
ARNHEM LAND

ARNHEM LAND

•Beswick Creek

SPIRITS OF PLACE

This section is about certain spirits which inhabit the land. They are generally earthbound and confined to one locality unlike the ancestral beings featured in the previous section, who appear to be present across vast tracts of country. Most of the images in this section are depictions of mimi spirits, as seen on rock walls in West Arnhem Land. Mimis live mostly in rocky crevices, which accounts for their stick-like appearance. They dare not venture out on windy days for fear their long thin necks will snap off, and only appear on windless days and nights to hunt. They taught the original Aboriginal people of this area of Arnhem Land the laws and customs, how to hunt and prepare kangaroos for cooking as well as paint and perform ceremonies. Despite their delicacy, they have magical powers: they float above the ground rather than walk and are reputed to raise and lower the roofs of caves to paint their own images, which inspired Aboriginal people to paint on the walls themselves. But they are not always helpful, or endearing. They can be mischievous and downright dangerous.

Mimi stories are told around the camp-fire at night. Their exploits are often used as a means of reinforcing good behaviour by exposing the scandalous behaviour of some of these beings and its often devastating consequences. Parents use the presence of mimis in the surrounding bush to discourage children from straying, in much the same way as the threat of 'the bogey man will get you' is used elsewhere in Australian culture. They are known to lure people away to their caves and such temptations can only be resisted by Marrkidjbu or magic-men. Only the wisest of Aboriginal elders are believed to have seen them.

As well as mimis carved in wood and painted on bark, the following images include Yawk Yawk, water spirits also from West Arnhem Land and a city artist's personal interpretation of guardian spirits in papier mâché.

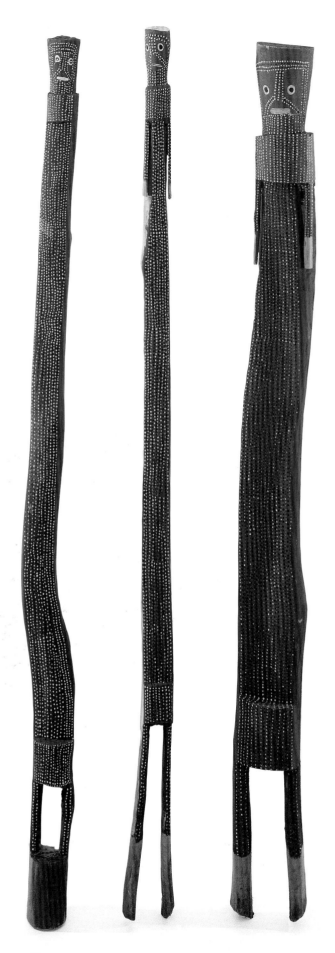

Left
Crusoe Kurdal
Mimi Figures
1985
Plate 22

Right
Samuel Wagbara
Three Mimis Dancing
1964
Plate 23

Crusoe Kurdal
Mimi Figures

Like their painted images, these carved mimi figures are extremely tall and thin. The largest is over three metres tall. The taller and thinner the better, according to the artist, because they are then better able to fit into the cracks of rocks. These carvings are related to the images found in large numbers in the rock walls of Kakadu and the Arnhem Land escarpment as well as being a popular subject for bark paintings. The figures are first painted with red ochre and then decorated with rows of white dots applied with a stick. They are used for ceremonial purposes as well as being produced for sale. Crusoe lives and works in Maningrida, an Aboriginal settlement at the mouth of Liverpool River on the coast of Central Arnhem Land. He is the sole inheritor of the rights to produce these innovative figures from his father, the late Crusoe Kuningbal, who was one of the most prolific early carvers of mimi figures.

Samuel Wagbara
Three Mimis Dancing

The three animated mimi figures on this early bark from Croker Island contrast markedly with the more static figures typical of Crusoe Kurdal's carvings. Although the images are similar, these express concepts relating to sexual misbehaviour (suggested by their enlarged sexual organs). They also feature ant-like heads and internal patterns in the x-ray style typical of rock art from the same region.

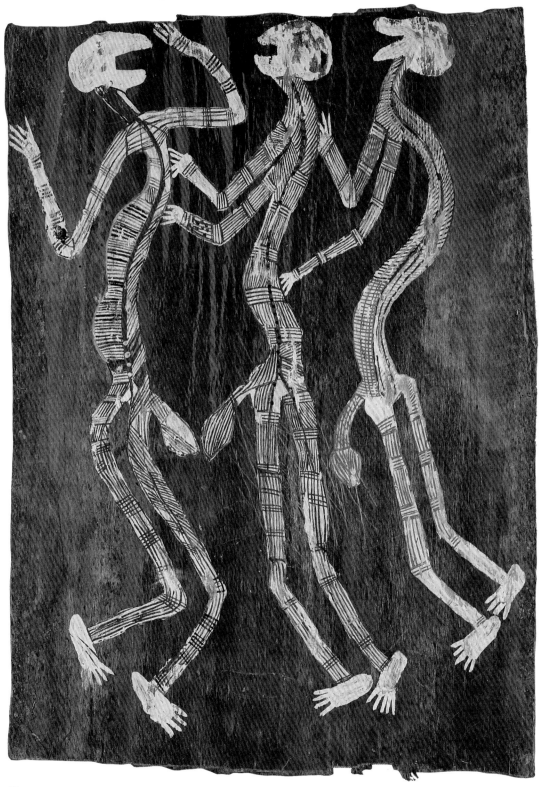

23

Anchor Barrbuwa Wurrkidj
Mimi Hunter and Corroboree

Anchor Barrbuwa Wurrkidj
Mimi Hunter and Corroboree
c1961
Plate 24

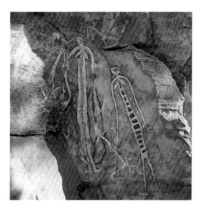

Kakadu National Park
Photo Dennis Schulz

The most distinctive feature of this bark painting is the rare glimpse it gives us of mimi spirits in their natural habitat, near the caves of the rocky sandstone West Arnhem Land plateau. These mimi spirits are the shy, harmless variety that flee at the approach of strangers into their rocky hideaways. They blow on the rocks and open cracks (seen here as red lines) allowing them to slip inside. A mimi hunter is shown carrying a wallaby across his shoulders and a barbed spear in the other hand, while in the background, more animated figures are engaged in a ceremony. One is seated playing the didgeridoo (sometimes called a drone pipe) close to a clapstick player who is keeping a rhythm for the dancing mimis above. 'Clever men' sometimes befriend the mimi and are taught their songs and dances. In their parallel world, they use the same kinship terms and speak the same language as the local Aboriginal group.

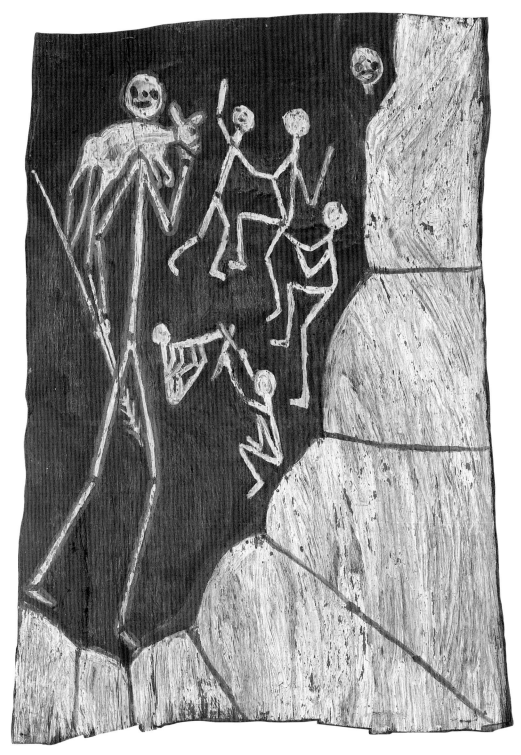

24

Jimmy Njiminjuma
Yawk Yawk

Jimmy Njiminjuma
Yawk Yawk
1985
Plate 25

Yawk Yawk, shown here as a water spirit, is part of a Dreaming cycle related to the daughter of the original creator, Yingarna, the Rainbow Serpent. These spirits are also known as 'young girl spirits'. The daughter's name was Ngalkunburruyaymi, which is sometimes used interchangeably with the term Yawk Yawk. They live in specific sites and are particularly associated with a place known as 'Dreaming Ladies' which is on a creek off the Liverpool River, west of Maningrida. These mysterious beings are usually shown with a woman's torso and often have a fishtail. Here, Yawk Yawk's flowing hair has become the trailing blooms of green algae or water weed found in waterholes, rock pools and creeks in the stone country. In fact, the water weed is described as Ngalkunburruyaymi's transformed hair. It has been said that the small creatures in the water – like the larvae of dragon flies – are a visible form of these spirits who metamorphose and fly away, and at other times, walk on land. The Kunwinjku people believe that 'clever man' can take these spirits as wives.

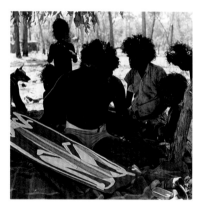

Jimmy Njiminjuma painting a lightning spirit on bark in his camp near Oenpelli.
Photo Penny Tweedie N.T. 1978

Yawk Yawk has strong graphic appeal due, in part, to the way the simplified image fills the space and creates interesting contrasts between spaces and the bold patterned areas. Like the preceding images, the strong linear quality, powerful whites and monochromatic palette of natural ochres is related to the rock art tradition of West Arnhem Land.

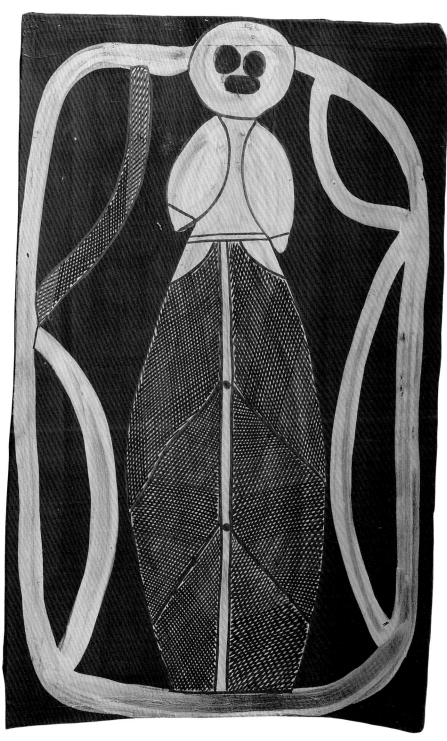

25

Judy Watson
the guardians, guardian spirit

Right
Judy Watson
the guardians, guardian spirit
1986/1987
Plate 28

Top
Judy Watson
Inside the rock
1988
Plate 26

Bottom
Nicholas
Spirit in the form of a skeleton
1960
Plate 27

"I've just been thinking about Aboriginality – all of us carry a sense of that being some part of our lives, our history, our parentage. When we do not look visibly the stereotype of an Aboriginal person we are assumed to have no 'identity'. We are the invisible ones..."

These shadowy, half-revealed ancestral figures entombed in life-size, plywood cut-outs were made by the artist in Victoria in 1986 and finished in Queensland the following year. She began with one form and ended with five, a number which occurs in her work in many different manifestations. Away from her family and country, Watson was creating her own guardians. The female shapes recall her matriarchal family that connects her with her Aboriginality through her mother, grandmother and grandmother's mother. The other shapes have been interpreted by some to represent her missing relatives. (Her grandmother was taken away from her people, the Waanji, of northwest Queensland.)

In Watson's country, bones were ochred, wrapped in bark and placed in burial chambers along the cliffs and gorges. Some of these sites were desecrated while others remain intact. The artist is attempting to reveal some of the concealed history of Aboriginal people in this country.

The tactile quality of the surface and the mark making reveal an intimate contact with the work: the feathered marks made by hand-rubbing pigment into the wood and the delicate tracery of lines. Wax, shellac, oil and water-based materials are used throughout the work. Behind the front figure, an image has been carved out of the wood. This was inked and hand-printed onto the transparent material which is suspended above the forms like a 'guardian spirit' (not pictured).

Nicholas
Spirit in the form of a skeleton

Nicholas is from the Mayall language group which is located around Beswick Station, near Katherine, in the Northern Territory. This x-ray version of a seated spirit in skeletal form was formerly used in burial ceremonies. It is a relatively old image, rarely seen today, however this way of representing figures was often used to show a spirit 'sitting' at a place, inhabiting its home.

The work Inside the rock (at left) by Judy Watson shows a seated spirit skeleton in a burial chamber which is strikingly similar to the Mayall image by Nicholas. These images, from different areas, decades apart and from Aboriginal artists with different backgrounds demonstrates the continuing tradition of Aboriginality. Watson, whose image is in pastel on canvas, has no particular knowledge of this old image in ochres on bark.

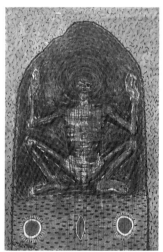

26

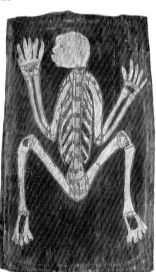

27

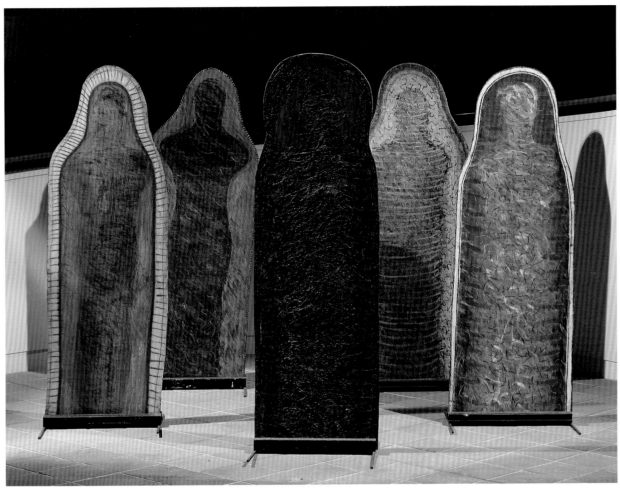

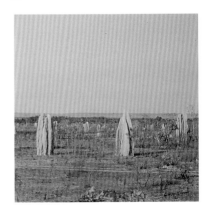

Left

This photo shows ant-beds in the northern part of Australia which bear a resemblance to Watson's sculptural forms. It is believed by some groups that ant-beds contain the spirits of deceased people.
Photo Yaja, Ramingining 1993

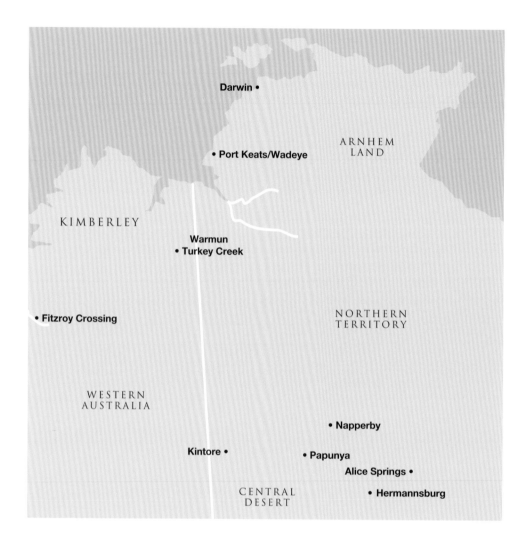

LANDMAPS

The works in this section have in common their cartographic focus as maps of the artists' land, painted with 'country in mind'. Sometimes they are topographical or geographical; at other times they are cultural or historical; usually they have elements of all four aspects. These are not the maps one associates with the measurement of distance, nor are they landscapes in the western tradition based on appealing views of nature.

In "traditional Aboriginal culture there is no such thing as nature without culture."[1] Instead nature – in this case, the landscape of the artist's country – is depicted as a kind of three dimensional map. The actions of ancestral beings are indelibly imprinted in the shapes of natural features, the colourings, textures and the topographic dimensions. The land, like the paintings that represent it, is a map of ancestral journeys and events, a map of Dreamings. The word for painting in many Aboriginal languages is synonymous with the expression 'my country'.

Unknown Artist
A map of Groote Eylandt

Unknown Artist
A map of Groote Eylandt
c1948
Plate 29

This enigmatic shape painted nearly 50 years ago by an unknown artist has all the characteristics of a map of Groote Eylandt: square in shape with capes, bays and outlying islands. Although the island is shown in aerial view, it is unlikely the artist viewed it from a plane. Rather, it shows a fisherman's or hunter's intimate knowledge of the contours of his island home, using the traditional Aboriginal artist's characteristic view from above. At the same time this shape may be a representation of the sea eagle or kestrel, an important totem, which is found in other bark paintings from the same period. It also bears a resemblance to depictions of the north winds drawn in the shape of the sails from the Macassan praus which for centuries sailed into the region on the northwest wind. Aboriginal people incorporated many aspects of Macassan culture and technology into their art, religion and lifestyle.

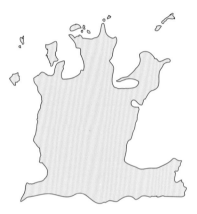

Contour Map of Groote Eylandt

—

29

Clifford Possum Tjapaltjarri and Tim Leura Tjapaltjarri
Warlugulong

Clifford Possum Tjapaltjarri and Tim Leura Tjapaltjarri
Warlugulong
1976
Plate 30

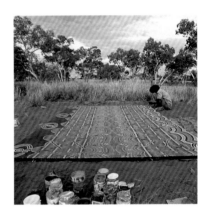

Clifford Possum at Mbunghara, N.T.
Photo John Corker c1986

Clifford Possum Tjapaltjarri is a custodian of Possum Dreaming sites on Napperby Station about 250 kilometres northwest of Alice Springs. It is through this association that he acquired the name 'Possum', which in Anmatyerre was also the name of his paternal grandfather. Clifford Possum was perhaps the first Western Desert artist to see the parallel between ceremonial sand paintings and European maps. His brother, Tim Leura shared this idea of combining a number of Dreaming stories in topographical relationship on the canvas.

This work is considered one of the most complex paintings ever produced by a Papunya Tula artist.[2] Few paintings from the desert could say more about the vitality and richness of a landscape pronounced empty and lifeless by those who refer to it as the 'dead centre'.

Warlugulong is more complex than a topographical map, showing also a variety of vegetation and land formations. It reveals the layering of a number of stories and a complex network of Dreaming tracks.

Warlugulong is the Anmatyerre language name for a site near Yuendumu where Lungkata, the old Blue Tongue Lizard man, punished his sons. The sons speared a kangaroo, but did not share it with their father as Aboriginal law decrees. In their long absence, the father suspected this, and the more serious infringement of killing and eating a sacred kangaroo for which the penalty is death. He set the bush alight and it exploded into flame, as seen in the centre of the canvas. Fire flicked out like the Blue Tongued Lizard's tongue. The footprints of the fleeing sons (who perished in the fire) are seen in white.

Another story shown in this work, tells of two carpet snakes who travelled from the clay pan lake country and two carpet snake men who instructed people in ceremonial matters at various sites which are seen as a string of concentric circles traversing the painting. Yarapiri, the Great Snake is depicted by the sinuous line at the top left, which is the snake's

travelling route from Winparku, 200 kilometres west of Alice Springs. Patches of white near the edge of the painting indicate that he travelled through limestone country.

The tracks of an emu ancestor from around Napperby Station are shown in white on the left side. On meeting a group of emu men from Warlpiri country, he invited them to his home in the east and shared its plentiful supply of bush berries and fruits, thereby establishing good emu country and introducing visiting patterns and ceremonies between different language groups.

The series of unlinked circles on the right-hand side of the painting tells the wedge-tailed eagle story. Along this route fled a terrified euro (hill kangaroo) disturbed from his peaceful browsing in the Aileron area. He sought sanctuary in rocky outcrops shown by the circles, but the eagle relentlessly pursued him and attacked, its beak tearing as talons struck – shown by one set of talon marks where the eagle landed. The euro died at the site marked by the top circle on the right.

The possum men's tracks meander all over the canvas with the tail mark dragging in between. They fought mala hare wallabies at Yalkuti. After the conflict, the possum men returned to the red gum trees lining the creeks and the mala to their sand and spinifex plains.

Sets of human footprints converging from the top left and right represent two groups of women who came, respectively, from central Warlpiri country and from the Aileron district north of Alice Springs. As they travelled, they danced in celebration of the prolific bush tucker.

The relationship of one site to another may not necessarily conform to the mono-directional system used by western map makers. The canvas is painted flat on the ground and artists move around it to start new Dreaming stories or simply to re-enter the work from a new position. As they do so, the north/south axis changes. It is analogous to the artist 'spinning in space above the landscape'.[3] "See, I put story first and (then) different patch of colour. You can see'm from the plane." [4]

An annotated diagram of Warlugulong can be found on page 142.

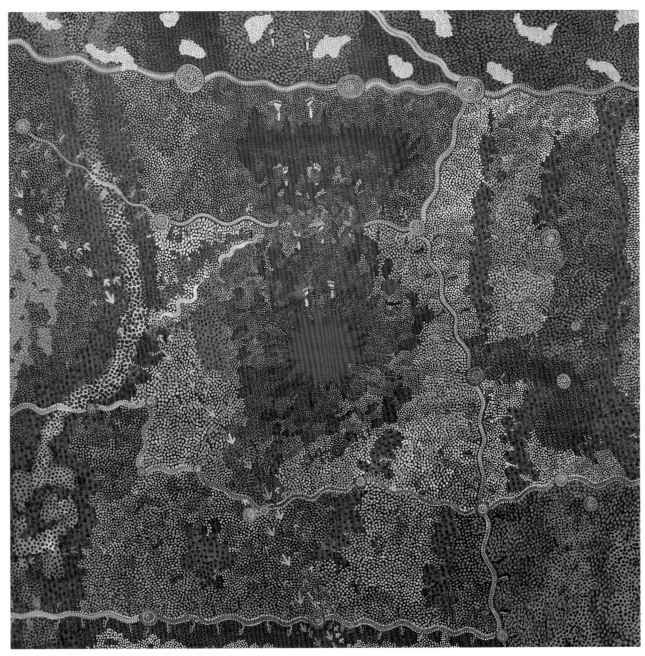

Albert Namatjira
Palm Valley

Albert Namatjira
Palm Valley
1940
Plate 31

"We have two ways of painting: sand painting and landscapes. For all of us they both have the same Dreaming story. This landscape painting we do, it shows the country. We don't just paint anything, that's not our way." [5]

Albert Namatjira painted his own country in a European style, using the technique taught to him by artist Rex Batterbee in 1936. He crossed cultural boundaries and became the first nationally prominent Aboriginal artist.

While it may look like a conventional European landscape, Palm Valley is also a map of Namatjira's land, showing the formations created by ancestral beings as well as special markings understood only by the artist. The central placement of the sacred waterhole girded by curtains of rocky cliffs creates a stage-like effect for an ancestral drama that would have been replaying in Namatjira's mind whilst painting this view of his country.

Despite the apparent European influence, a closer examination of the painting reveals many similarities with the early Western Desert 'dot' painters: a desert palette of oranges, rust, sand, purplish-blues and deep blue black shadows; a circular site marker, and a sense of having "been composed in from the edges yet extending beyond the frame resulting in an overall symmetrical tension across the surface". [6] The western eye accustomed to focusing in the centre of the composition is directed to the activity around the edges, normally an out-of-focus peripheral zone. There is little evidence of the golden mean so integral to the European landscape tradition and the one-point perspective has been tilted to allow more detail. The repetition, overall patterning and sense of space are consistent with an Aboriginal vision. The fact that four decades elapsed between the time this work was painted and the time it was purchased by the Gallery in 1986 reflects the view that prevailed until recently in the 'High Art world': that Namatjira's paintings were derivative and not 'real Aboriginal art'.

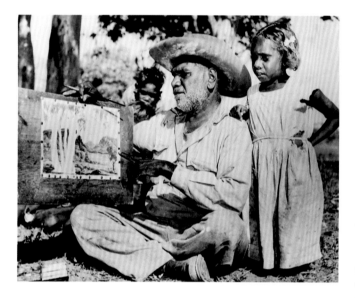

Albert Namatjira with his grand-daughter Jillian Namatjira in the Chewings Ranges circa 1954.
Reproduced courtesy of
Advertiser Newspapers Ltd, Adelaide

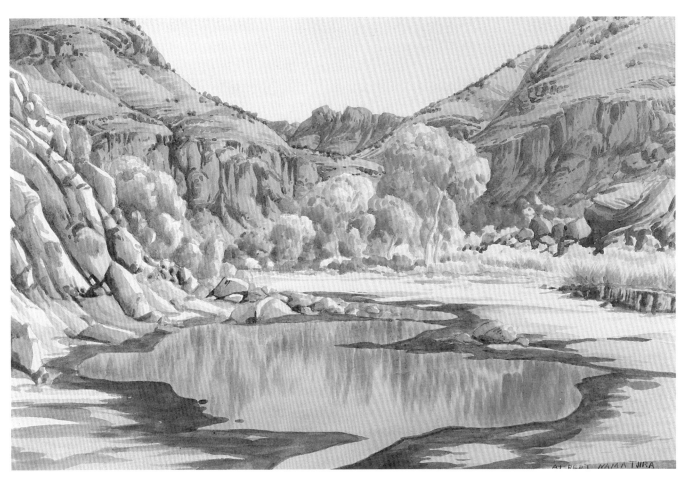

31

Ronnie Tjampitjinpa
Untitled

Ronnie Tjampitjinpa
Untitled
1994
Plate 32

"When we think of Ronnie Tjampitjinpa we should not evoke the romantic notion of a tribal Aboriginal living in the remote deserts of central Australia untouched by the outside world. Think more of a man roaring across thousands of miles of country in his four wheel drive with his spears strapped to the roof rack and paintings in the back." [7]

This description helps place a traditional elder and artist like Ronnie Tjampitjinpa realistically into a contemporary context.

Ronnie has been a member of the Papunya Tula Artists' Company since its beginnings in the early 1970s and more recently has been gaining recognition as one of Australia's foremost abstract painters. However, his bold and uncompromising paintings are not abstract art, but powerful expressions of an attachment to his country and culture. They also reflect his relationship with the contemporary Australian art world and bear a visual resemblance to the work of the Minimalists and the Op artists of the 1960s, but Ronnie's source of inspiration and intentions are a world apart. He draws on potent Pintupi icons, condensed into almost abstract terms.

These highly-charged fields of energy, placed on a diagonal axis, are a variation on his previous works, which were generally more formal and restrained. Like stones breaking the surface (tension) of a waterhole, a rippling effect sets in motion a pulsating action. The squares transform into circles which contract in the middle and expand beyond the edges of the canvas. This push-pull motion is intensified by a palette based on the traditional red and yellow ochres and black and white, combined in alternating bands of contrasting tones.

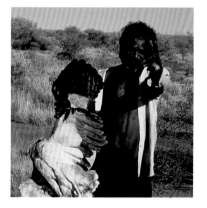

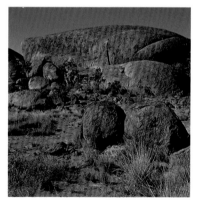

Top
Ronnie Tjampitjinpa with bush turkey, Marawa near Kiwirrkurra, W.A.
Photo John Corker 1990

Bottom
Ronnie Tjampitjinpa's country just south of Kintore.
Photo John Corker 1991

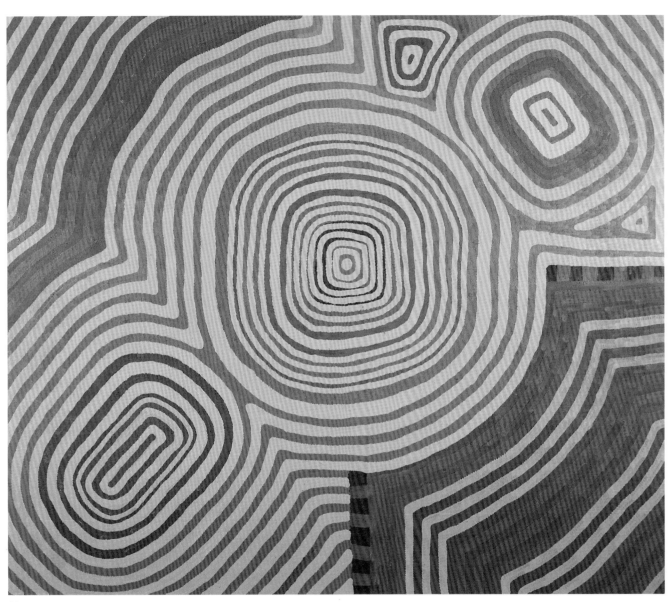

32

Willy Tjungarrayi
Tingari Story

Willy Tjungarrayi
Tingari Story
1986
Plate 33

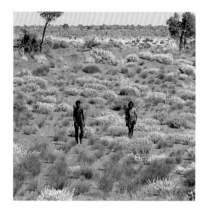

The travels of two young Tjungarrayi men near Kiwirrkurra.
Photo John Corker 1990

Willy Tjungarrayi began painting for Papunya Tula Artists in 1976, and is one of the company's senior artists. As a young man, he travelled hundreds of kilometres east from the desert to settle around the Haasts Bluff ration depot, and from there moved to Papunya. He and his family joined the move back to the Pintupi homelands, settling at Kintore in the early 1980s. As a ritual elder, Willy has the status to paint the most significant parts of the religious cycles.

This classic work maps the journeys of the Tingari, a group of ancestor beings who travelled over vast stretches of country performing rituals and creating and shaping particular sites. The Tingari Men were usually accompanied by novices, and their travels and adventures are enshrined in a number of song cycles. These mythologies form part of the post-initiatory instruction of young men today. The Tingari ceremonies are of a secret nature and no further information was given by the artist. Tingari Story is one of Willy Tjungarrayi's largest canvases, and took many months to complete. The artist was assisted with the background dotting by fellow Pintupi artists, including John and Simon Tjakamarra whose styles are clearly discernible from Tjungarrayi's hand on the painting. The artist included a vast array of sites in the painting, which depicts his country in the region of Lake McDonald. In mythological times, a large group of Tingari Men made camp in this area on their journey from the Peterman Ranges towards Kintore.

Viewing this work is an extraordinary visual experience. The surface expands and contracts in accordance with the viewer's changing distance and angle of vision, with a 'bulging' effect in the centre of the painting caused by the bigger spaces and bolder lines. The eye dances over the glowing surface in perpetual motion, an idea in keeping with the continuity of the spiritual cycle that informs it.

The artist would have been in an elevated state of mind as he traced his knowledge of the ancestral landscape onto the canvas. Power invested in the work is felt through the tension created by the restraining net of interconnecting Dreaming tracks, stretched across the vast surface like a cultural grid.

The painting's perspective is more like the view from a satellite than a plane. From a distance, the white dots in the centre of the concentric circles glow like a star map suspended above the muted browns and the blacks of the desert at night. This cosmological dimension also includes the idea of 'as above, so below'. Below the surface of the land reside the ancestral powers, whilst above the ground their previous existence is indicated by a tracery of journey lines and sacred sites, which function as guidelines for Aboriginal people.

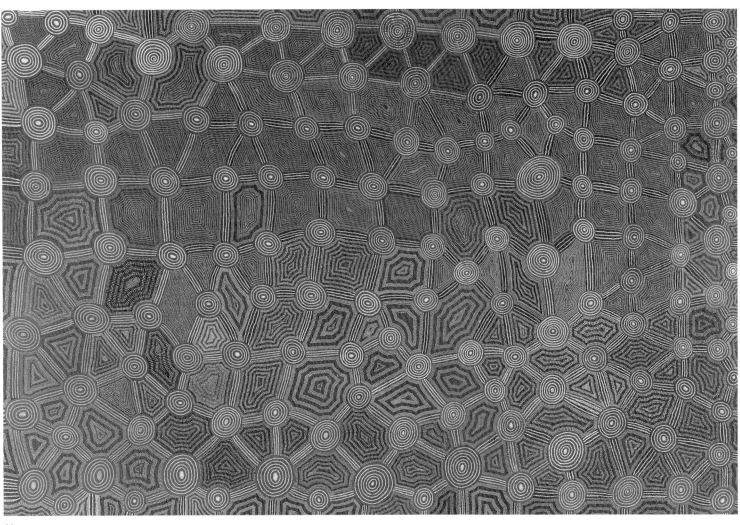

33

Cory Surprise Wakartu
Jilji

Cory Surprise Wakartu
Jilji
1991
Plate 34

This is one of a series of paintings by artists from the Karrayili Education Centre painted for The Art Gallery of New South Wales and presented by the Fitzroy Crossing community as representative of their art.

"This is <u>Jilji</u> (sandhills) in my country, my country's name is Pilmarr. The jilji is in the centre of the picture. The shapes around the edges are pamarr (rocks) and waterholes. In this country there is a lot of red desert sand. Jilji are the sandy ridges in this country. These are billabongs and jumas (waterhole). There are dead trees near the billabong. This is the country where I was born. I was taken away when I was very young..."

Cory Surprise is one of a group of women from Fitzroy Crossing who has recently been introduced to painting on paper with acrylic paint. She was a student at Karrayili, an Adult Education Centre established in 1982 by the community as a gathering place for adults for the purpose of Law and Education. Although the paintings originally produced by the students were part of the literacy program, they have eclipsed that original function. Cory Surprise now paints with the Mangkaja Arts Resource Agency at Fitzroy Crossing, which began in 1991. Jilji is an excellent example of how Cory Surprise and other students have begun to record, in paint, sites of their country in the Great Sandy Desert by listening to the stories of elders. During the early 1960s these younger people were removed to pastoral stations.

"I was born in the desert. I never saw my mother and father. They died in the desert. When I was crawling age I went to Christmas Creek station... All our family who were already living at the station gave us clothes. We were all frightened. The station manager was hitting people so we ran away. The police tracked us down and put chains around the men... Then I worked at the main quarters for the police, collecting eggs and washing plates."[8]

The ease with which Cory Surprise handles the paint over large surfaces is related to smearing paint onto bodies for ceremonies. With her flattened palm she employs the same approach to her paintings, giving them a tactile quality. She uses similar 'flourishes' of the hands to describe her work. The energy radiating from the surface comes from a combination of vibrant primary colours on floating forms against white spaces, overlaid with flickering dots. This map of land is essentially an aerial view with shifting perspectives. The variegated mark making shows the different forms of vegetation and land formations.

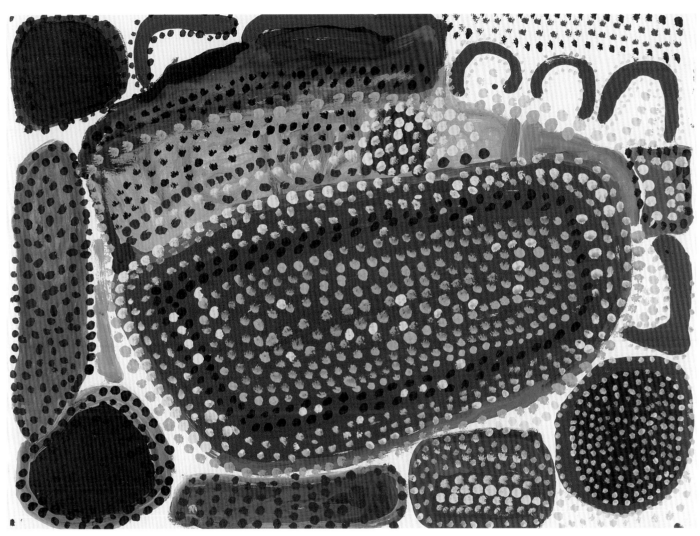

34

Rover Thomas
Ngarin Janu Country

Rover Thomas
Ngarin Janu Country
1988
Plate 35

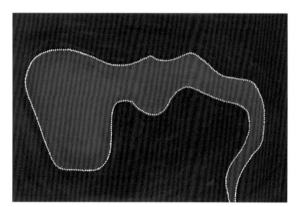

Rover Thomas
Cyclone Tracy
1994

Within one prolific decade, Rover Thomas has made his mark in Australian art history with a vision of ancestral themes expressed in a distinct abstract style. Rover's success quickly gave impetus to a painting movement based around Turkey Creek in the Kimberley region of Western Australia.

As a painting Ngarin Janu Country is harsh, sparse and haunting. The dark shape which dominates the surface hovers like an ominous, brooding presence. It delineates Rover's country, from above as well as vertically, scarred by the gouging actions of large-scale mining and massacres and denuded by pastoralists. This is not a map of a land that is animated by ancestral journeys and coloured by a profusion of new growth, but rather a map of a topography that is both geological and historic, an ancient land that has witnessed human interaction and suffered ignoble treatment.

The stark beauty of this painting is assisted by the limited range of natural ochres that sink into the canvas, giving an earthy resonant warmth. These broad areas of black and brown are contoured by strings of white dots similar to the dots used in West Arnhem Land, just as the planar view of broad areas is a feature of desert art. These similarities are not surprising, since the Kimberley region borders on the Western Desert to the east and Arnhem Land to the northeast.

Cyclone Tracy, which destroyed Darwin on Christmas Day 1974, acted as a catalyst on the remote communities of northwest Australia who recognised this natural phenomenon as a sign from the Great Rainbow Serpent. The Serpent is particularly associated with cyclonic weather. This event awakened in Rover and others a need to keep their culture strong and resulted in ceremonies of which paintings like this were originally part.

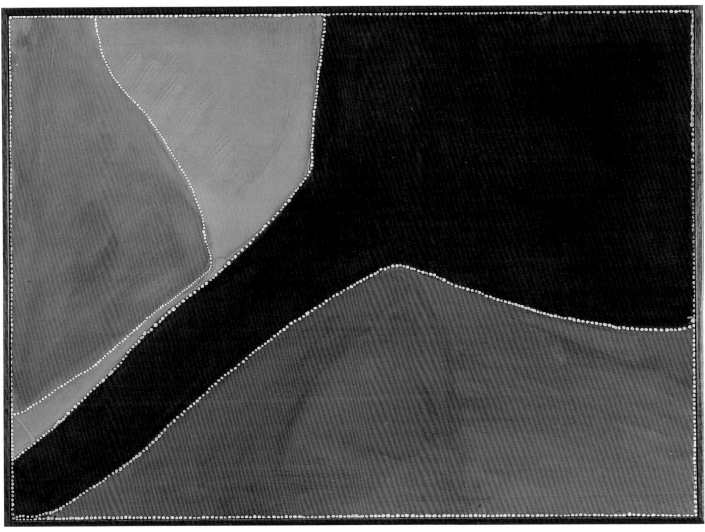

35

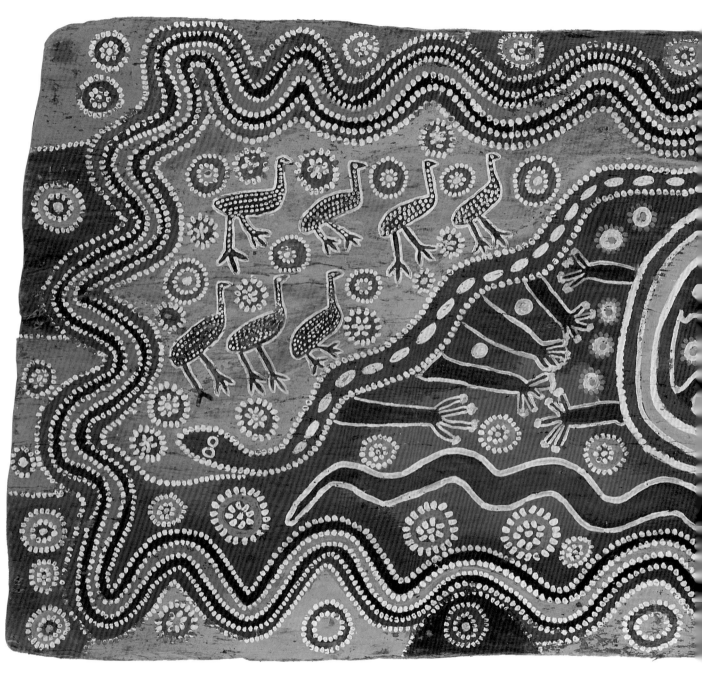

36

Nym Bunduk and Kevin Bunduk
Emus Feeding
1961
Plate 36

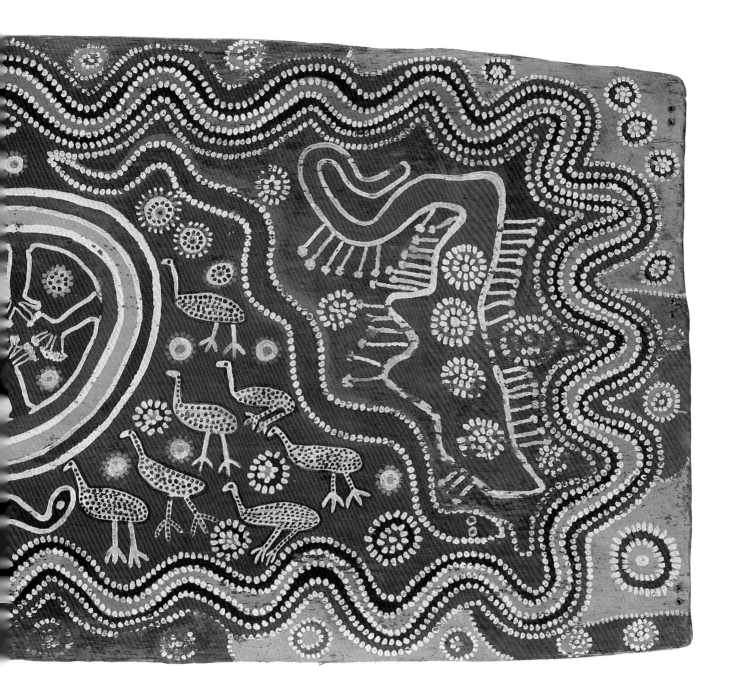

Birari
The Creation of Five Waterholes

Birari
The Creation of Five Waterholes
c1961
Plate 37

Birari and Nym Bunduk of the Murrinpatha language group, along with others of their generation, experienced a period of intense conflict and dislocation with European settlement, but were later responsible for restoring and spreading cultural and religious ideas in the Port Keats (Wadeye) region. Dreaming stories, revealed to them by ancestral spirits, are the source of their art.

This land map, painted in natural ochres on bark, shows an area of significance for the artist. It is seen from above and, not only records the presence of important waterholes, but describes how they were formed by ancestral beings.

A number of spirit pythons came from Victoria River and travelled north to an area south of Port Keats, where they created the large water-hole in the centre called Tapun. This is linked to the four waterholes, in each corner of the painting, which were created by the two snakes shown on either side. The water-courses linking the corner circles to the most important site, in the centre, are shown parallelling the bodies of the writhing water snakes. These radiate like zigzags of lightning from central source of power, but at the same time, there is a sense of the slow rhythm of water in the meandering movements of the snakes as they follow the water-courses.

Port Keats art often incorporates features of art from surrounding regions. The dark plain background, naturalistic images and the use of dots to divide spaces is similar to techniques used in bark painting from West Arnhem Land. The free use of line also relates it stylistically to rock art from the region east of the Ord River, encompassing the lower reaches of the Victoria and Fitzmaurice Rivers. The influence of desert art further south can be seen in the use of aerial views, concentric circles and linking pathways or 'journey lines'. Unlike less disrupted areas of Arnhem Land, designs like these do not necessarily have a long lineage in Port Keats.

Nym Bunduk and Kevin Bunduk
Emus Feeding

Emus are seen feeding in the dry season on stunted flowering foliage (see plate 36). A creek has been reduced to a circular waterhole, shown in red with water lilies and bottle trees growing on its edge. There are three water snakes, (the female with eggs inside her) and their offspring. Around the edges of the painting is a creek with yellow water, black mud banks and high red ground adjacent.

The 60s was a period of experimentation in Port Keats, and artists in the area renewed artistic activities after prolonged disruption. They experimented with new combinations of natural ochres, creating in this example, the greens and pumpkin tones of the dry season. In combination with black, we see the burnt ground, a common sight during this season.

There are unexplained images such as the unusual bladder shape with spokes on the left. Aboriginal people in the area today say they recognise the style of the particular artists, even the place depicted, but they are less certain about the meaning. It is also possible that 'outsiders' are only given limited information.

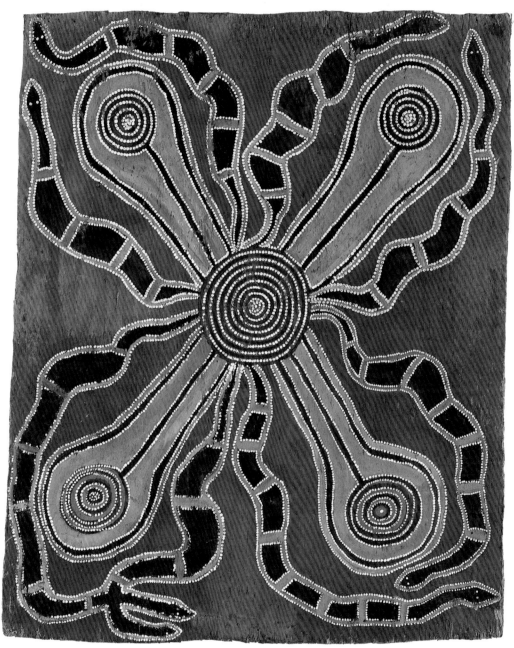

37

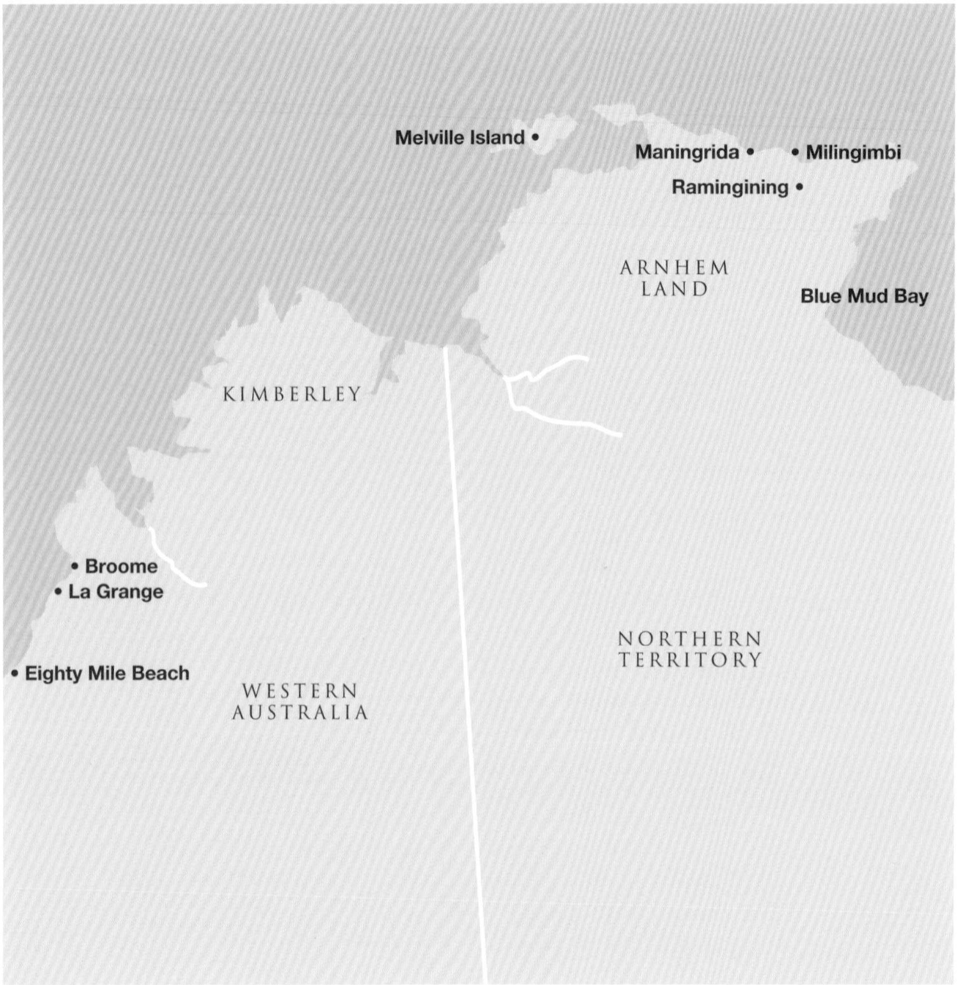

Melville Island •

Maningrida •   • Milingimbi

Ramingining •

ARNHEM
LAND

Blue Mud Bay

KIMBERLEY

NORTHERN
TERRITORY

• Broome
• La Grange

• Eighty Mile Beach

WESTERN
AUSTRALIA

SORRY BUSINESS

'Sorry business' is an expression used widely around Australia by Aboriginal groups for everything associated with the death of a person. It includes mourning, preparation for ceremonies and funerals, obligations and taboos. It reflects the human response and is well-understood by those living in traditional Aboriginal societies and those in urban environments in southern capitals. The word mortuary, which is the more commonly used term to describe works depicting death and associated ceremonies, conveys a western sense of their finality. In the Aboriginal understanding of death, like that of many cultures around the world, it is a state of transition between life and rebirth in an unending cycle. This concept is embodied in the pukumani ceremony which is performed around specially prepared grave posts. The ceremony purifies the area, protects the relatives and assists with the progress of the spirit to another level of existence.

David Malangi's bark painting Gunmirringu funeral scene depicts the first of a different funerary ceremony for the Manharrngu people of Central Arnhem Land which is performed to assist the passage of the soul to its various destinations.

Renewal, an aspect of this cycle of rebirth, forms the basis of the Morning Star Ceremony as the daily appearance of this star suggests.

Pukumani Grave Posts
Melville Island

Various Artists
Pukumani Grave Posts
Melville Island
1958
Plate 38

This spectacular collection of Aboriginal grave posts comes from Melville Island, some 200 kilometres north of Darwin, in the Northern Territory. Commonly referred to as the 'Pukumani Poles', they were acquired in 1958 by the late Tony Tuckson, then Deputy Director of The Art Gallery of New South Wales. Since their installation at the Gallery in 1959, the Pukumani Grave Posts have been the centrepiece of the Aboriginal art collection. Each stage of the production of the 17 posts was documented by the late Tony Tuckson and Dr Scougall, for historic and artistic reasons. These notes and images are derived from their work. [1]

Although it has become synonymous with the grave posts, the word pukumani refers to the burial ceremony (the poles themselves are called tutini). Pukumani also prescribes behaviour for those connected with the deceased. This includes certain taboos about touching particular people, food and objects.

The first pukumani ceremony was organised by Tokwampini, the Honey Bird man. Its subject was Purukuparli who died after avenging his son's death which was caused by his wife's sexual misbehaviour. When the ceremony was performed, Tokwampini instructed the ancestors in the laws of marriage and social behaviour. They then dispersed and metamorphosed into various forms of fauna, heavenly bodies and ritual objects. This ended the creation period.

The Tiwi people of Melville Island see the poles as representing aspects and characteristics of the deceased whose grave they surround. [2] Alone and insecure, the dead person's spirit or mopaditi seeks to rejoin its family and is potentially dangerous to surviving kin. Not until the climax of final ceremonies, which can occur anytime up to one or two years later, does the spirit finally depart to join other relatives in the spirit world. The participants camouflage themselves with body paint and false beards to avoid recognition by the spirit who may cause them harm.

The carved forms and painted motifs on these Pukumani Grave Posts symbolise the transition from life to death. Each grave post represents the recently-deceased person beginning to decay. As Paddy Freddy explained in 1986 "... pukumani designs are to make posts like people."[3] The posts with shapes that resemble heads are said to be female whilst the projecting 'arms' of other posts indicate male gender. Two distinctive projections may symbolise the raised arms of a man, buffalo horns or ears or the jaws of a crocodile, none of which are mutually exclusive. Certain motifs in the designs depict rope, wire, fingers, eyes and body scarification and relate to the clan group and territory of the deceased.

As a result of being separated from the mainland by treacherous straits, the art of the Tiwi people has developed in relative isolation and is characterised by the highly patterned, geometric designs seen here. It features broad criss-crossed diagonal and zigzag lines, arcs, circles and rectangles on areas divided into panels. In more recent times, these designs have been reproduced on paper and fabric using gouache and printing inks.

The Grave Posts are carved and painted by artists, with the greater proportion of the work being carried out by Laurie Nelson, One Eye (Tuki-al-ila), Big Jack (Yarunga), and Bob One (Gala-ding-wama) assisted by Big Don (Burak-madjua) and Charlie Quiet (Kwang-dini). Within the confines of the tradition, there was a marked individualism in their approaches. Big Jack worked long hours slowly building up his complex designs with great care, whilst Bob One who was more vigorous in his painting,

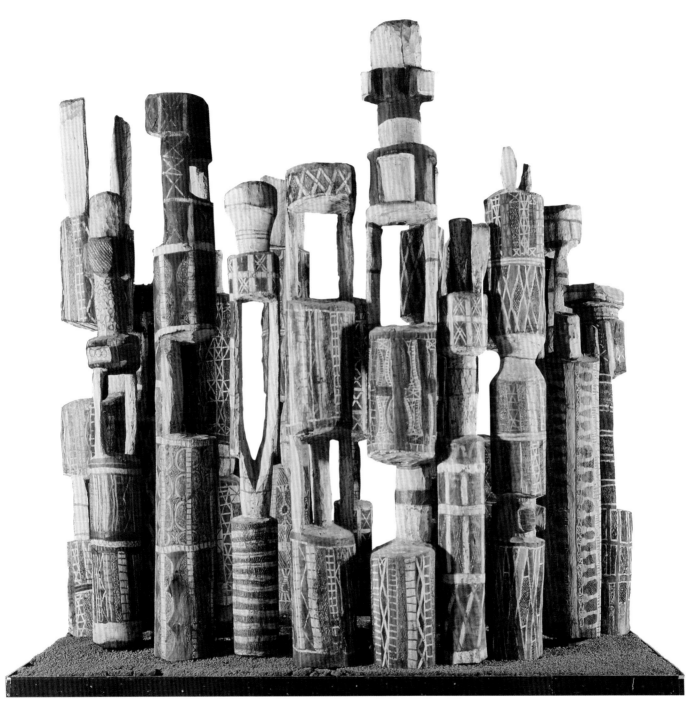

38

scored his white lines, and generally relied on more marked contrast of black and white, using yellow and red sparingly. The geometric designs on the uncut surfaces contrast with the white of the cut areas, enhancing the sculptural quality of the posts. Views through the apertures create new spaces and patterns. Bark baskets painted with similar designs are traditionally placed over the top of the posts. These are used to carry food for the carvers or to carry payments (presents) at the end of the ceremony. At other times, they are used to contain the belongings of the deceased before they are burnt.

The seventeen posts are arranged as if around a grave site. Such a number, in a traditional context would indicate that the deceased was an important person. A child might receive a single pukumani pole. The deceased person's relatives commission the posts through a middle-aged man of high status. Poles of outstanding quality and originality receive high payment.

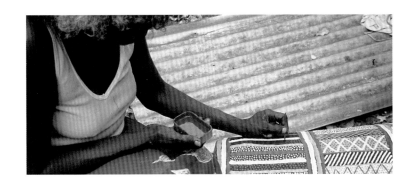

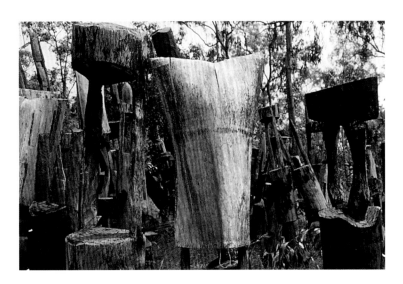

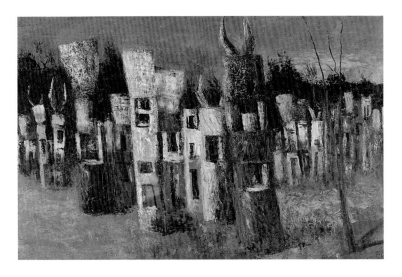

The poles in progress

1 After felling the 'bloodwood' eucalyptus tree, Bob One cuts it to the required length, strips the outer bark and carefully decides on how the wood will be shaped and where the initial cuts will be made. Work must proceed quickly, because the timber hardens as it dries. Most of the carving is done in the wet season, when high humidity slows the drying process. The grave posts should be cut from living bloodwood or ironwood trees, so as to 'bleed' into the ground. The carver requires considerable skill, starting with full-bodied swings and gradually shortening his grip and swing to trim the area to the desired shape. In the past, stone axes, mussel shells and fire were used to fashion the posts. Shark skin or stones were used to smooth the surface in preparation for painting.

2 Laurie and Big Jack burn the post over a fire until the surface is dark brown or black. To furnish a binder for the paint, the crushed leaf (Anacardiacea – buchanania obovata) from the mango family is dipped in water and rubbed on the post. (Sometimes soap and other alternatives are used.)

3 Bob One collecting white clay on Melville Island near Snake Bay Settlement. Other natural pigments used are yellow and red ochres. They are mixed to a paste in a tin, though formerly a shell was used.

4 Bob One chewing a gum twig to shape as a brush. These are made from twigs of various sizes by crushing and chewing the ends. The false beard and face paint camouflage the participant, so that he is unrecognisable to the spirits of the deceased (mopaditis) present near the burial site.

5 Big Jack painting the undercut section with white clay.

6 Big Jack painting the lower section of the grave post.

7 Big Jack using a wooden comb (boita) to apply dots

8 Laurie feeding Big Jack. It is the duty of the pukumani group to feed the workers while they are cutting and painting the posts. Food caught or gathered by the pukumani men and women is cooked and placed in the bark baskets for the 'workers'. It is taboo for others to eat this food.

9 Big Jack painting a post on Melville Island.

10 Bob One with a completed grave post. He is wearing an orange goose-feather ball on his chest. The false beard and simplified facial design symbolise Pintoma, the barn-owl woman who assisted her husband Purutjikuni, the boobook owlman, at the first Kulama ceremony – an associated life-giving ceremony.

11 A group dancing the pukumani, variously adorned and reflecting animal totems associated with the myth cycle.

12 Tony Tuckson wrapping the post first with fabric followed by a paper bark padding.

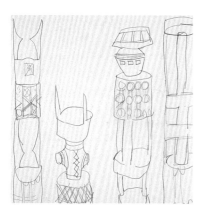

Top
A detail from a page in Tony Tuckson's sketch book 1958.

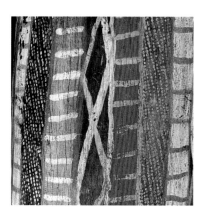

Bottom
Detail of designs on the Pukumani Poles.

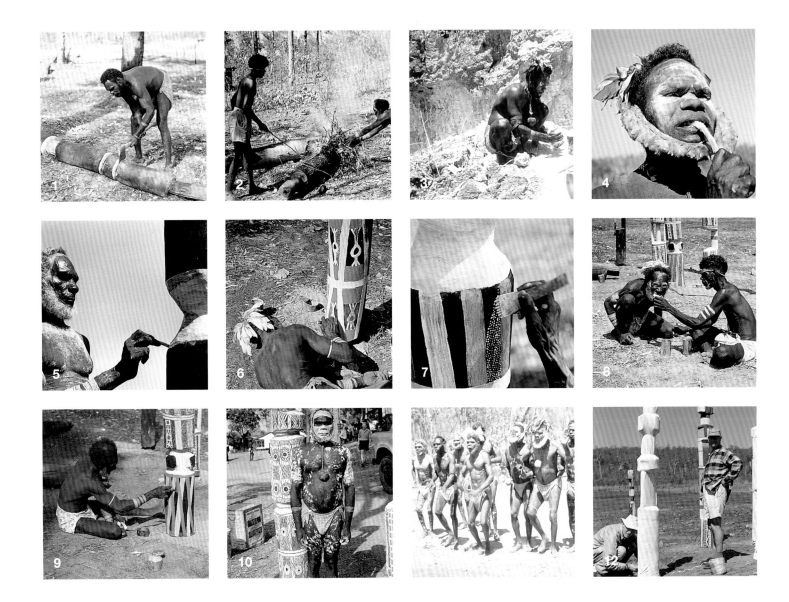

Mau
The Morning Star Ceremony

Right
Mau
The Morning Star Ceremony
1960
Plate 40

Below
Philip Gudthaykudthay
Badurra and wooden Mindirr
Hollow Log Coffin and Dilly Bag
1985
Plate 39

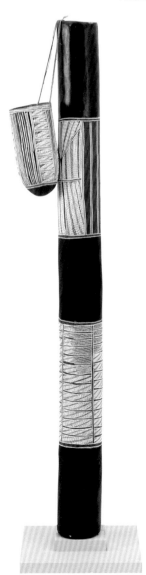

Mau is from Blue Mud Bay in North East Arnhem Land. The Morning Star ceremony belongs to the Dhuwa moiety and tells of an old woman who lives on the Island of the Dead (which does have a geographical location) and keeps the Morning Star captive in a basket, tied to a long string. Each morning before dawn, she releases it to travel across the sky on a route named by the singers of the ceremony. It lights the land and carries messages from the departed spirits to their clansmen and women as they are awakened by the first bright rays of light. Just before the sun rises, the old woman reels in the Morning Star and keeps it in the dilly bag until the next morning.

In Mau's painting, the dancers of the ceremony are shown as two lines of white figures on either side of the ceremonial ground. This is also a representation of the Morning Star pole which has three strings attached to the top for the dancers to hold. At the conclusion of the dance, the strings are returned to the three positions in the sky commonly occupied by the Morning Star, which appears before dawn. The consent of the two spirit figures (depicted on their island above the dancers) is always necessary for the strings to reach the Morning Star. A yam, the food of the spirits, is shown horizontally at the top like a string of black lozenges. On the right are two men on an island and the brother of the Djang'kawu Sisters, in a canoe. Also shown are brolgas, water snakes and a dingo. The cross-hatching represents dust from the dancing which is kicked up to block the sun, bringing dusk and allowing the night to fall.

Today throughout Arnhem Land, many related ceremonies take place. Although collectively termed 'friendship' ceremonies by some observers, they are more precisely 'rituals of diplomacy' performed to maintain good relations between neighbouring groups. Different clan groups call these rituals by different names, Banumbirr being the most well-known.

Philip Gudthaykudthay
Badurra and Dindin (wooden Mindirr)
Hollow Log Coffin and Dilly Bag

"There is a little creek near there (Gatji Creek) and in that creek is where the first hollow log ceremony took place for the Dhuwa people. They say that this is where a crow made one of these logs... this is painted with a design, like a body design... The log is thought of as the flesh, and the skin, and putting the bones inside is like putting the soul back into the body... the soul is indestructible. It stays behind."

The hollow log coffin and dilly bag are traditionally used in funeral ceremonies called Bukubot to contain the bones of the deceased. The grid design refers to the artist's country at Gunyungmirringa, which is a relatively flat forested landscape near Hutchinson Strait between Howard Island and the mainland. It is also the landscape associated with the ancestral exploits of the Wagilag Sisters, one of the major creation stories of Arnhem Land. In this work, Gudthaykudthay tells the story of one of the episodes in the religious cycle. The black sections on the log refer to the crow who conducted the first ceremony over the bones of his sisters. He then carried the log full of bones up into the sky, and spilt them across the black night sky forming the Milky Way. It has been said that the cosmological dimensions include references to the black hole and the coal sack as well as to constellations in the form of a dilly bag. At one level, the red ochre symbolises the blood of the ancestors, while white refers to bones and yellow to body fat. The fine cross-hatching or rarrk is the artist's clan design, the use of a silvery white and brilliant yellow ochre, and the resultant shimmering effect associated with spiritual power are characteristic of Gudthaykudthay's work.

Hollowed naturally by termites, the bone pole forms the second and final stage of the funeral ceremony which could occur up to three years after the person's death. Bones are crushed and put into the dilly bag (dindin) then ceremonially taken out of the dilly bag and thrown into the hollow log. Wak Wak the black crow plays a part in this ceremony. The hollow log is then placed in a public place and left to the elements.

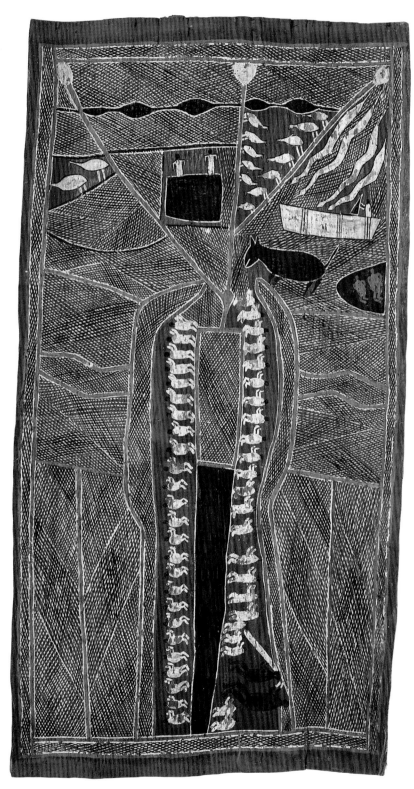

40

David Malangi
Gunmirringu funeral scene

Right
David Malangi
Gunmirringu funeral scene
1983
Plate 41

Far right
David Malangi
Gunmirringu the great hunter
1983
Plate 42

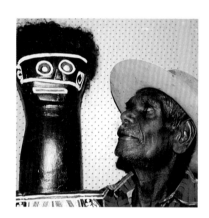

David Malangi
admires Gunmirringu.
Photo Yaja 1993

David Malangi is a senior ritual leader and custodian of three tracts of land on either side of the Glyde River, near Ramingining in Central Arnhem Land. The area is of great significance and this work is part of a series of land rights barks which Malangi painted to assert his (and his people's) ownership.[4]

The funeral ceremony for Gunmirringu the Great Ancestral Hunter is performed to assist the passage of the soul to its various destinations in preparation for rebirth. Death represents only one stage of transition, one level of spiritual existence.

"He (Gunmirringu) is staying there and looking at the areas and around him the Raga or Wurrumbuka tree (white berries). It represents the death of one of the clan. When we have that body we go and collect these white berries – still today... This is what happened to him long ago. They (the singers sitting playing clapsticks) are sending out the people to collect bush potatoes (blood yam)... Even in those days maybe because the people died of Darrpa Snake (King Brown Snake). That's why the spirit is there because of that snake..."[5]

The word 'Gunmirringu' means 'the first people' and refers to the great ancestral hunter shown in the centre. Although he appears to be standing, he is actually lying in state and is the subject of the very first funeral ceremony for the Manharrngu people which is taking place around him. His clansmen are seated with clapsticks, singing ceremonial songs and dancing, and the deadly King Brown Snake or Darrpa which bit and killed him is shown alongside. (see plate 46 for an image of Darrpa). Around Gunmirringu are the takings of his last hunt: yams (rongi), nuts and the butchered kangaroo which refers to the death of a person. The dissection of the carcass symbolises the exhumation of the human bones in preparation for re-burial in a hollow log coffin.

The story of the life and death of Gunmirringu is owned by Malangi and represents the Manharrngu mourning rites. The song cycle associated with this ceremony is performed when a member of this clan dies. Gunmirringu's spirit is the major guardian spirit of the people and is seen today as a rock in the sea just off the mouth of the Glyde River.

As with many cycles, the images are cues to complex repetoires connected to other cycles. This story is associated with the Morning Star Ceremony (see plate 40) and the Island of the Dead which is the final resting place of Gunmirringu's spirit. The flowering stringy bark is analogous to the tasselled strings of the Morning Star pole which represent the stars and symbolise life and rebirth. Similarly, the berries refer to the stars on the poles. These trees are also a reference to the white berry bush under which the hunter sat to cook his food when the snake struck. The diver duck and black crow are also strongly associated with this mourning cycle.

Malangi's painting style is highly individualistic, characterised by broad fluid lines and creamy dots. His rich warm brown ochre is rarely used by other artists in the region. In contrast to the central circular style favoured by most Central Arnhem Land artists, he prefers to use a vertical composition. The Gunmirringu story depicted on one of Malangi's early barks received some notoriety after it was recreated on the first Australian dollar bill in 1966.[6]

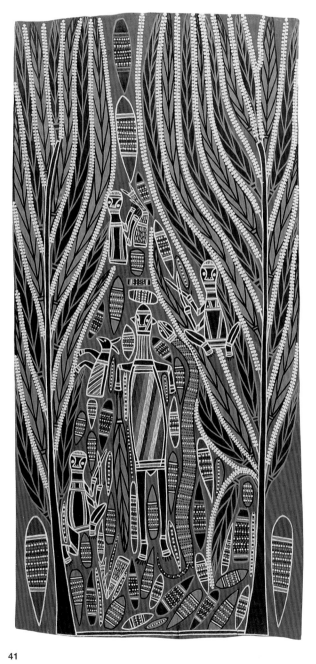

41

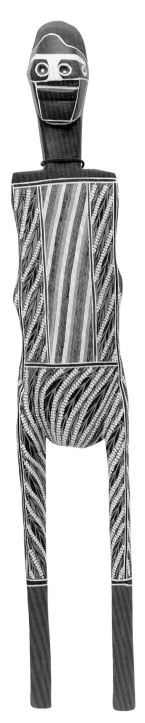

42

John Dodo
Maparn (Doctor Man)

Mathew Gilbert
Head

Right
John Dodo
Maparn (Doctor Man)
1985
Plate 44

Below
Mathew Gilbert
Head
1985
Plate 43

'Big' John Dodo as he is known locally, and Mathew Gilbert are from La Grange, south of Broome in Western Australia. They started carving sandstone heads in the 1960s. Dodo became a master carver of these heads and passed his knowledge on to other receptive artists from this region. He was previously renowned for his finely executed engraving work on wooden objects and pearl shells. For several years Lord McAlpine, whilst resident in the area, stimulated the production of these carvings for his collection. Since his departure from the area, they are rarely produced.

These two heads, coloured with natural ochres, are representations of Maparn, meaning Doctor or 'clever person'. John Dodo was commissioned to begin carving these figures by an elder who had a revelation in the early 1960s. In this visitation, a rayi spirit named Walkarurra taught the elder a new ceremony or marru and instructed that two human heads representing Walkarurra be carved out of soft wood. They were to be displayed upright in mounds of sand and were to be shown to all at the conclusion of the ceremony.

Dodo had the privilege of creating the first two figures. On their completion, the ceremony was presented to the community, who embraced it enthusiastically. Encouraged by this reception, Dodo experimented further, producing heads of mud, clay and stone. Stone became his preferred medium and the popularity of this kind of work spread amongst other artists in La Grange region. Although employing new techniques and styles, these works, like many in the Kimberley region, retain links with the past and draw directly on the Pukarrikarra or Dreaming.

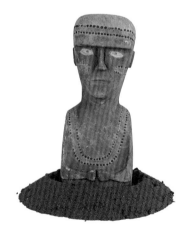

43

The visitation received by the elder, also told of a family from ancestral times who were hunting near Eighty Mile Beach, or Payarr. The young son killed a female goanna heavy with eggs and ate them – an act which was taboo. This angered the Pulanj, the rainbow serpent who sought revenge first by unleashing violent storms and then by setting out to devour the boy. However, the boy's father was a medicine man and had the power to seal the cave in which his family took refuge to withstand repeated attacks by the serpent. Enraged and with gaping jaws, it attacked the mountain itself, biting off large chunks of rock. This continued throughout the night whilst the petrified family huddled inside. Finally at dawn, the Serpent withdrew and the rain stopped. It is these chunks of rock that John Dodo uses to carve the images of the medicine man. The power of the Maparn is captured in Dodo's finely sculptured head of blackened sandstone which shows a traditional hairstyle and headband framing an intense and sombre face. Gilbert's more roughly carved bust of the Maparn shows ceremonial markings.

These sculptures are among the last sandstone heads to be produced in this area of the Kimberley. The Art Gallery of New South Wales was fortunate to receive a recent gift of 39 heads by 14 different sculptors from Lord McAlpine's collection.[7] The two heads pictured will mark the end of the journey through the new Yiribana Gallery, just as they marked the end of a ceremony. These works, made exclusively by male artists, are the most recent additions to the Gallery's Aboriginal art collection.Coincidentally, the very first acquisitions were also sandstone carvings – those presented 46 years ago – made by female artists on the eastern side of the continent.[8] Such quirks of history breathe life into a collection.

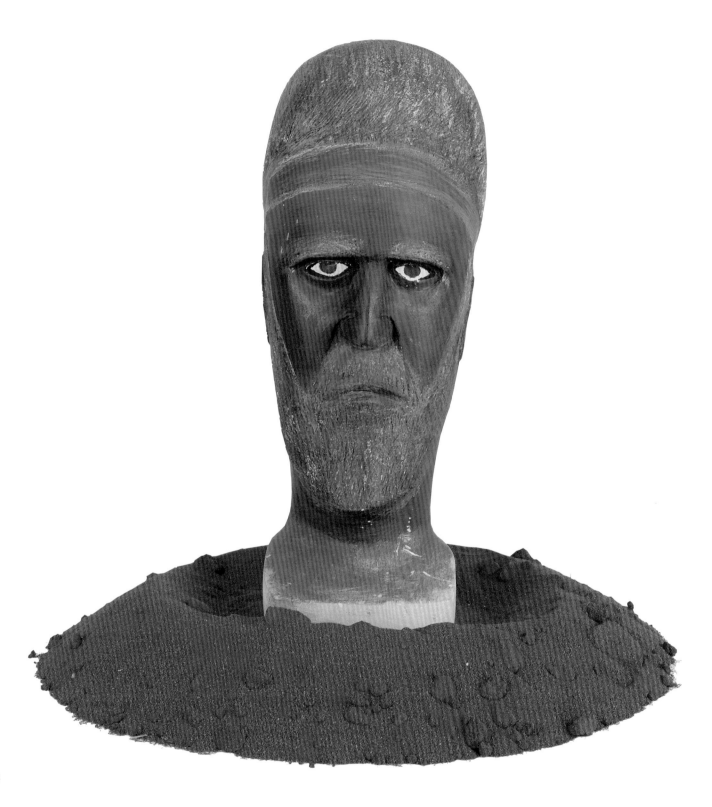

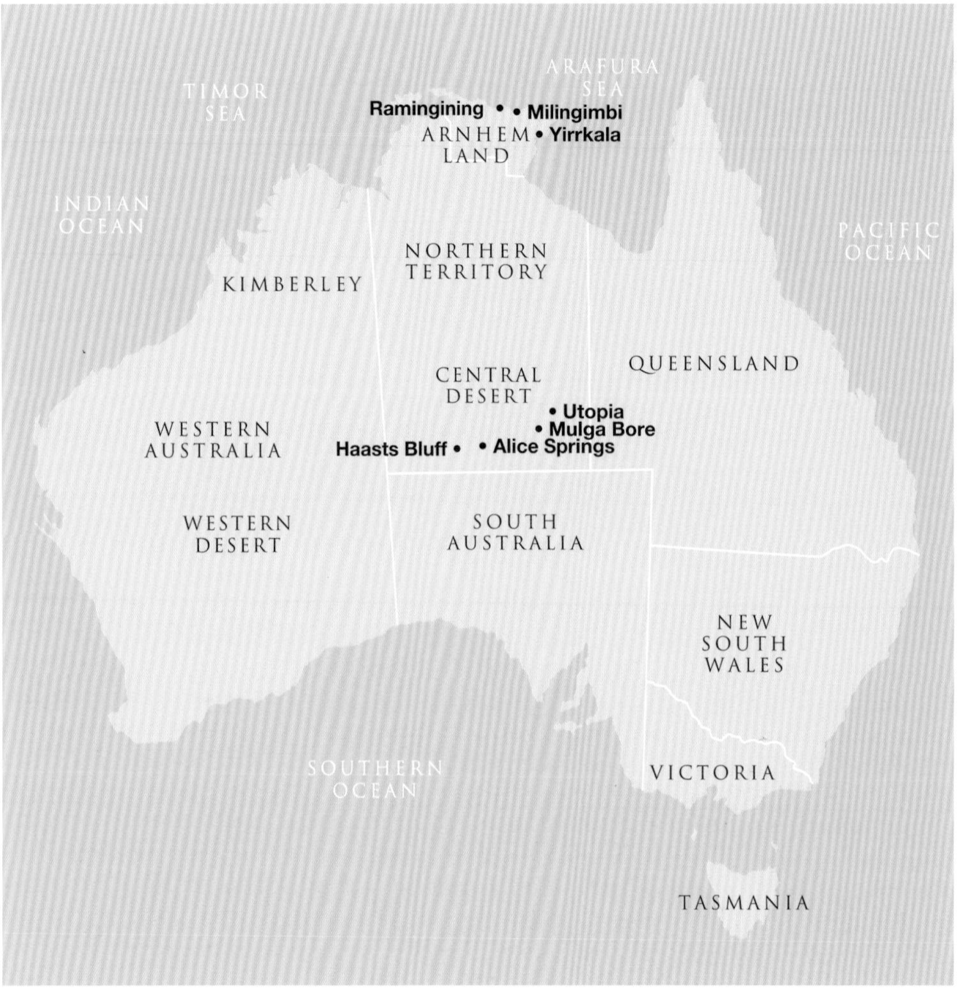

TIMOR
SEA

ARAFURA
SEA

INDIAN
OCEAN

Ramingining • • Milingimbi
ARNHEM • Yirrkala
LAND

PACIFIC
OCEAN

KIMBERLEY

NORTHERN
TERRITORY

QUEENSLAND

CENTRAL
DESERT

• Utopia
• Mulga Bore
Haasts Bluff • • Alice Springs

WESTERN
AUSTRALIA

WESTERN
DESERT

SOUTH
AUSTRALIA

NEW
SOUTH
WALES

SOUTHERN
OCEAN

VICTORIA

TASMANIA

SHIMMER

The desire to produce a visually vibrating surface is the aim of many Aboriginal artists. It is a means of investing the work with spiritual presence and elevating it from the ordinary to the extraordinary by evoking the power of ancestral beings. This practice is part of a continuing tradition that has its roots in ancient ceremonial practices of mark making on rock walls and bodies. Just as the special markings on the bodies of those involved in a ceremony help to transport them to another spiritual level, so particular markings on a painting perform a similar function for the artist in these works. The act of painting itself is a ritual activity in which the artist inscribes ancestral events in paint on canvas or bark. In many works, the spiritual fervour or contemplative state that accompanies the act of creating is an act of homage which also makes them religious icons, a form familiar to western audiences through their own traditions.

Access to a new range of vivid colours, new painting tools and new technologies have increased the artist's ability to find ways of creating the desired 'shimmer', the brilliance which expresses the spiritual quality of their work. The traditional cross-hatching (rarrk) seen on bark paintings and the dotting techniques of desert painters have been extended to include high-key colour combinations. Emphasis is on scale and simplification, as well as new ways of applying paint. In some of these works, paint is applied in a 'scumbling' of dots or dragged by the fingers across the surface as stripes as in body painting. In other works, dots have been applied with a fine brush or stick to form carefully patterned grids.

As 'flash' and showy as some designs may appear, they are rarely used for decorative purposes alone, although this may be part of a plan to attract attention in the first instance. They are primarily part of a greater spiritual experience and express a total world view in which every aspect of creation and behaviour is connected.

Gurruwiwi Midinari (Mithinari)
Djaykung – File Snakes
c1960
Plate 45

Gurruwiwi Midinari (Mithinari)
Djaykung – File Snakes

Midinari whose works are distinguished by
a rich variety of surface patterning, particularly
dots,[1] was a prolific artist from Blue Mud Bay,
North East Arnhem Land. Typically barks from
this area feature clan designs.

This monumental and elegantly proportioned
bark is nearly three metres in height. Its spiritual
power is evoked by the scintillating gold patina
that glows across the surface, enhanced by the
deep black shapes. The shimmer is achieved
through a brilliantly coordinated patchwork of
cross-hatching (rarrk), dotting and striping that
continually advances and recedes, drawing
the eye into the ancestral landscape below –
a landscape formed by the mythic actions of
the Great Python, Wititj.

The term 'painted literature' used in the past to
describe the primary function of bark paintings
is particularly apt for this work. It functions like
an encyclopedia explaining the various episodes
of the Rainbow Serpent's epic journey and the
symbolic references to moral conduct and the
cycles of nature. (see Land Before Time pp. 42-3).

The file snakes dispersed over the aerial
landscape are believed to be various manifestations of the Serpent associated with the
Wagilag creation cycle (see plates 18 and 19).
They have also been described as 'a harmless,
short, fat variety that are good to eat'. The
Wagilag Sisters' journey started in the region
of Midinari's country, and in this eastern version
different elements of the story are included.
After the Wagilag Sisters accidentally profaned
the waterhole of the Great Python, seen coiled
in the bottom half of the painting, the other
snakes gathered around the waterhole. On
hearing that the Python had swallowed the

Sisters, they coerced it to regurgitate them.
Two female snakes are shown around the
yellow oblong shape which refers to Gorimula,
a big rock submerged in the sacred waterhole.
The star shapes are waterholes fringed with
water lilies. These are not only important sites
in the story surrounding the central drama, but
are also the artist's personal totems. The circular
dot design, to which Midinari had sole rights,
is seen on the waterlily leaves and indicate the
presence of the Great Serpent at his well.

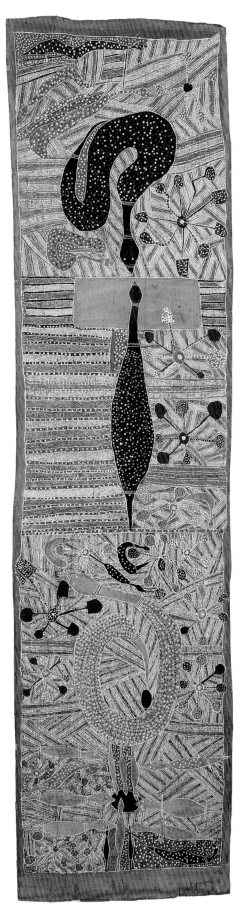

45

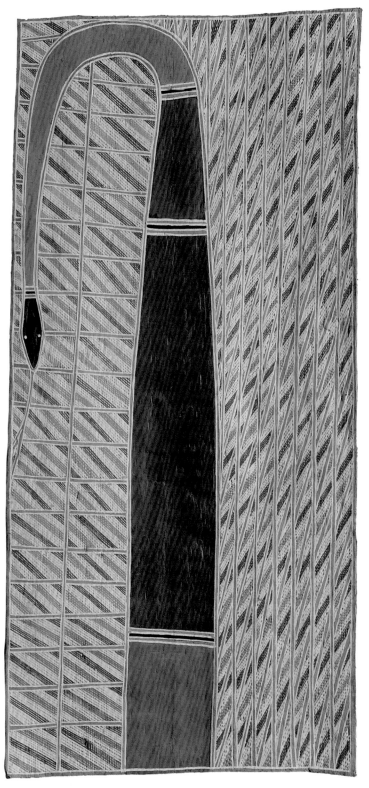

46

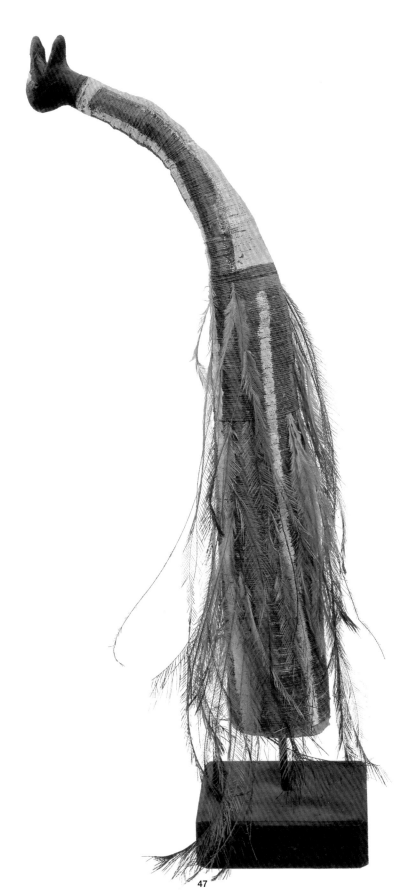

Left
Fred Nanganharralil
Darrpa, King Brown Snake
c1986
Plate 46

Right
Artist Unknown
Emu
c1956
Plate 47

47

Gungiambi (attributed)
Untitled
c1956
Plate 48

Fred Nanganharralil
Darrpa, King Brown Snake

This powerful bark painting by Nanganharralil is a fine example of the traditional use of cross-hatching or rarrk to create a brilliant shimmer (see plate 46). With a human-hair brush and natural ochres, the artist has laid down detailed blocks of high contrast pigment repeatedly to excite the eye. The optical impact is increased by the addition of a zigzag effect on the right-hand side and the stark contrast with solid bands of colour on the vertical shape of the snake beside it.

The flickering surface of golden light which seems to saturate the surface, befits the subject – the creative powers of the Great Serpent[2] – as it did in the previous painting (see plate 45). In this Central Arnhem Land painting however, the snake is isolated from the other elements of the story. The painting records a critical stage in the cycle when the snake reared up from its waterhole, arching its body across the sky to form a rainbow after the deluge. The atmosphere of the wet season is experienced through the shimmer of the slanting line pattern, left of the snake.

The different designs on either side of the snake are the clan designs of two language groups. As well as a kind of weather map, these markings also function as a land map showing Nanganharralil's wife's mother's country (Liyagawumirr) on the left and his clan country on the right (Djambarrpuyngu). References to these tracts of land suggest that the serpent was probably at the last stage of his journey in the Buckingham Bay area. The arching of the body, in this context, may refer to its final action before it disappeared underground forever. This graphic portrayal of the central form and the elegant simplicity of the composition enhances the spiritual quality.

Artist Unknown
Emu

The quintessential character of the emu is captured in this totemic representation from Milingimbi in Central Arnhem Land (see plate 47). Its long arched neck and open beak is further animated by a shimmering robe which resembles the quivering action of the bird in motion. This effect is achieved through the use of selected plumage from the emu and alternate stripes of yellow, red and white ochre. This work is constructed from a cylindrical cone of paper bark bound with vegetable fibre string into which the feathers are fixed. The head and beak are modelled in wax. It is a principal totem for the Gupapuygnu people and used in ceremonies. Participants mimic the prancing actions of the bird in dance.

Gungiambi (attributed)
Untitled

This old bark painting from Central Arnhem Land has a rare kind of potency. It refers to sacred aspects of the Wagilag Sisters' religious cycle which have been intentionally veiled with abstraction. The wet season and, in particular, the monsoonal deluge brought on by the Great Python, Wititj in the myth cycle are strongly evoked. There is a strong visual sensation of the movement of water: falling drops and driving rain, shimmering sheets of water across the landscape, and wave patterns or tidal marks in the central band. The organisation of these patterned panels achieves the kind of symmetry, balance and order that one associates with the Wagilag rituals, whilst the division into halves with one side mirroring the other, recalls the moiety structure of some Aboriginal societies.

As with art from any culture involving abstraction, one is able to respond to the visual qualities of the work without knowing the specifics of the artist's intention. The white linear pattern interrupted by bands of yellow, red and black stains recalls body designs. It is interesting to compare this with a similar visual effect on the emu totem with its striped string pattern and with the woven pandanus mats and dilly bags from this area. White dots punctuate the dark background, like stars in the night sky, giving it the cosmic dimension integral to these religious cycles. 'Abstract' paintings of this style are said to be no longer produced in this area.

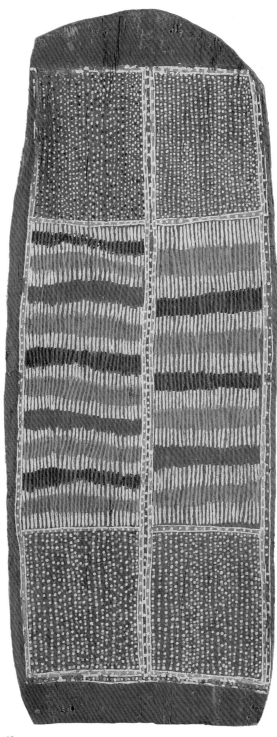

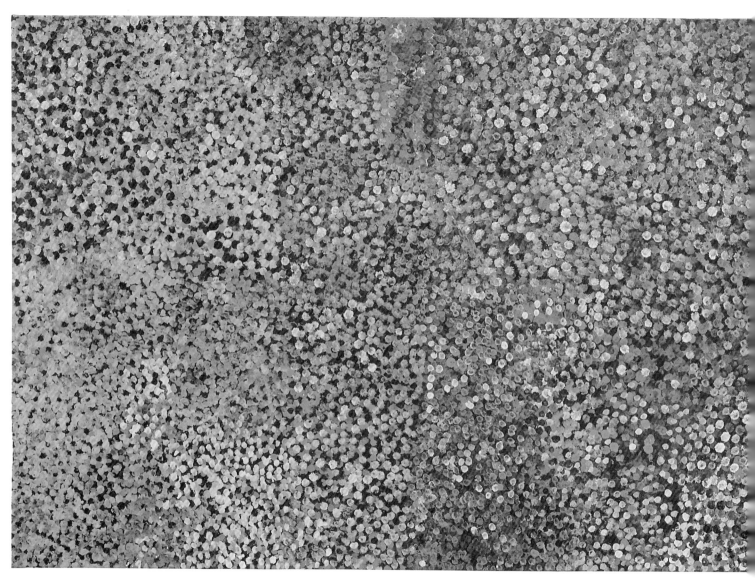

49

Emily Kame Kngwarreye
Untitled
1992
Plate 49

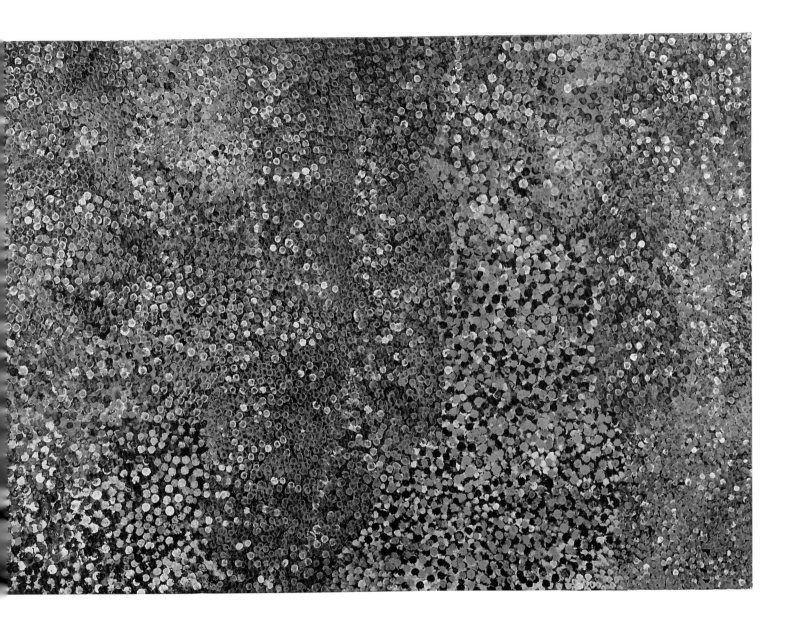

Emily Kame Kngwarreye
Untitled

Emily Kame Kngwarreye, a leading woman in Eastern Anmatyerre ceremony and ritual knowledge, is a great-great-grandmother and an award winning artist. Her skill and originality as a painter has resulted in her work being placed in major collections throughout the world.

When asked about her work, Emily explains simply, "This is my country, this is me". Her paintings are always about one story – the story of her country and everything which is important to her in it: bush food, seasons, animals, songs, wind and the dispersal of seeds recalled in seed Dreaming ceremonies. Emily's paintings encompass a total vision of her land. Her responsibility to nurture and care for it is enacted in the process of painting, just as it is in the associated ceremonies. Plaintive singing and displays of emotion usually accompany this journey in paint over ancestral lands. To view this work is to experience the rhythms of the Awelye ceremonies described as 'looking after country'. The heat and energy is 'felt' through the use of feverish earthy pinks and rust-reds, the swirling dust in the clouds of lighter tones, and the action of dancing bodies in a mosaic of gyrating finger-painted daubs. With eyes squinted, the viewer may imagine dancing figures which appear to emerge, singly on the right and in a massed group amidst swirling desert dust on the left. The undulating field of dots shifts in hue and density as the eye is taken into the rich landscape. From a distance the lighter dots appear to float to the surface, just as seeds float in the wind. The artist's middle name 'Kame' means 'seed pod'. Sensed, but not seen, are the feet in motion – the paddling action of women's feet upon grasses to release seeds – and the swaying rhythms of the winnowing and grinding processes.

A number of Emily's paintings reveal glimpses of striped patterns on breasts or Dreaming maps, associated with the seed dreaming cycles. It is characteristic of her work that oblique symbolic references are concealed beneath the layers of dots applied by finger, brush or stick. Her most recent works feature bold stripes dragged across the surface which are also based on breast designs.

Emily Kame Kngwarreye's use of dots reflects the batik work which she and many other older women from Utopia took up in the late 1970s. It was a natural progression for Emily from the layering of dots on silk to over-dotting on canvas (see plate 49). Before she discovered the lush fluidity of acrylic paint in the summer of 1988, Emily had been making marks in sand and painting on bodies to accompany storytelling throughout her life of more than 80 years.

Seasonal changes affect the artist's palette and temper the tonal and textural qualities of her work. She has captured the colour of the desert landscape, the oppressive heat and the deepening reds of the rocks in the late afternoon. This 'action' painting not only mirrors the abundant life and vitality of the desert not easily discernible to non-Aboriginal eyes, but also its vastness. The painting has no beginning, no end, and can be viewed from any direction reflecting the method of producing ground paintings in the desert where the artist works with the painting flat on the ground and enters it from all sides. However, unlike most desert artists, who work with stretched canvases, Emily usually passes the canvas across her lap, holding it close to her body and working one field at a time in the method of batik painting. It is a considerable physical feat to complete a canvas of the dimensions of this work, using this technique. It is the biggest canvas the artist has ever tackled and will be the last of these dimensions because of the physical demands on her advanced age. This painting is also remarkable because, according to Emily, it is the only one in which she has completed the whole life story of the seed Dreaming.

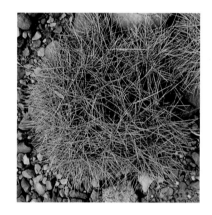

Above
The seeds of the spinifex
grass are melted to make a resin
and used as a binder.
Photo Christopher Hodges 1990

Right top
These boulders are
located near Utopia.
Photo Christopher Hodges 1993

Right bottom
Gloria Petyarre and
Emily Kame Kngwarreye.
Photo Sydney Morning Herald 1994

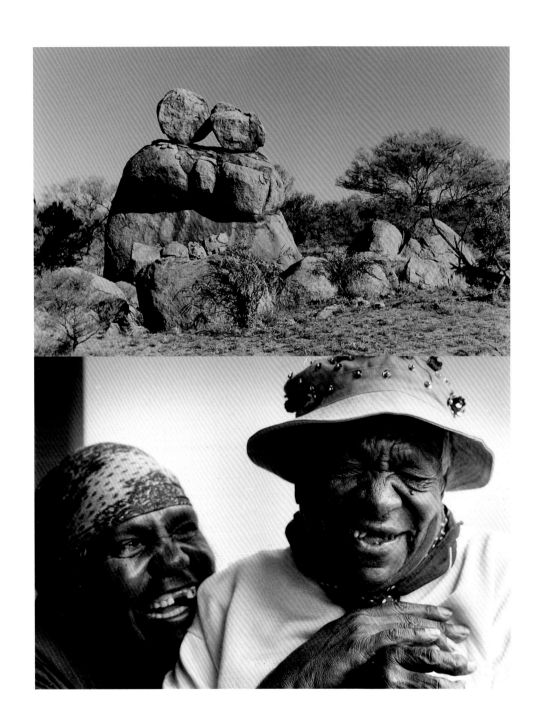

Ada Bird Petyarre
Awelye for the Mountain Devil Lizard

Ada Bird Petyarre
Awelye for the Mountain Devil Lizard
1994
Plate 51

Below
Katy Kemarre
Female Figure
1993
Plate 50

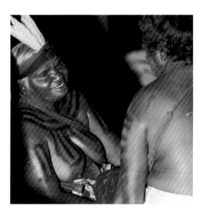

*Ada Bird and Gloria
Petyarre with painted breasts.*
Photo John Corker Alice Springs 1989

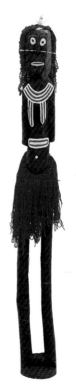

Ada is one of the leading senior artists from the Utopia community and is closely related to Emily Kame Kngwarreye. Like Emily, she is a great-grandmother who lives at Mulga Bore with her extended family. She maintains cultural links with her land, fulfilling her role of 'caring for country' through her painting and ceremonial activities. Katy, who produced the carving of the female figure, is also from the Utopia group of artists and lives at Ngkawenyerre, a site nearby.

This painting based on the body designs for Arnkerthe (Mountain Devil Lizard) is an excellent example of Ada's recent work. There is a meditative quality combined with a heightened sensuality. The eye is directed to the centre of the work by a mandala-like image which appears to reverberate with an endless source of power, from which lines radiate in ever-widening gyres to the very edges of existence. The contrasting blue and red curved lines shimmer, adding to the dynamics. The central roundel indicates the totemic dreaming place of the Mountain Devil Lizard, which would be the focus of the ceremonies referred to in this work. It also functions as the meeting place, dancing ring and camping places, of both the ancestral beings and the ceremonial participants.

Katy Kemarre
Female Figure

The specific images of breasts, and the patterns painted on them for women's ceremonies, emphasise the importance of the nurturing role of women in traditional Aboriginal society. They are the managers of the land and its resources, and they affirm this role through their ceremonies and paintings. This concept is reinforced in

Katy's female figure of a women decorated for ceremony. It also shows how ceremonial designs connect one art form to another. This is one of the first group of Utopia carvings to depict the ceremonial adornments so clearly: the hair string belt, the nose piece, the feathers and hair and the skirt of red wool. Red appeals because of its strength and luminosity which assists the artist in investing the work with spiritual power and status.

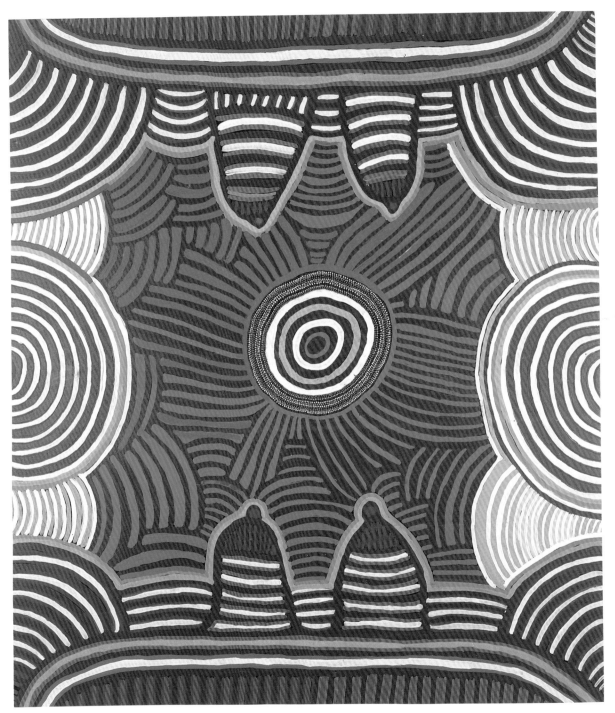

51

Mitjili Napurrula
Spears at Ualki

Mitjili Napurrula
Spears at Ualki
1993
Plate 52

*"Here is my father's dreaming that he told me.
His name was Tupa. I was a little girl... Today
I am painting his country. I'm just learning...
It's his Tjukurrpa (Dreaming) that I'm painting...
After I got married my mother taught me my father's
Tjukurrpa in the sand, that's what I'm painting
on the canvas."*

Mitjili and her brother Turkey Tolsen Tjupurrula paint their father's spear Dreaming, Tulpaku Tjukurrpa stories from his country on the other side of Kiwirrkura in Western Australia. It is a flat, sandy land with plenty of water.

Mitjili lives at Haasts Bluff, 230 kilometres west of Alice Springs in the Northern Territory, one of many places where communities have established centres to encourage artists and promote their work. The Ikuntji Women's Centre established in 1991 is responsible for the development of several artists whose vibrant spontaneous work is making an impact in the contemporary art world.

The strongly coloured stripes represent the spears against the desert sands. Highlighted with dots, they reverberate across the surface of the paper, giving a sense of the quivering motion of spears in flight. This work echoes the repetitions and rhythms of the land and the ceremonies that celebrate the patterns of nature.

Although a new artist in this medium, Mitjili has been drawing designs like these in sand and on other surfaces throughout her life. The direct application of paint by dragging her finger across the paper, revealing the underlayers, is similar to the effect of skin showing through stripes painted on the body.

Vivid colours in similar tones create optical effects reminiscent of some of the American Op artists of the 1960s. The visual stimulation fuses the sensory and the spiritual and signifies the ancestral power the artist has invested in the work. This procedure is related to the ground paintings, in which the power of the design is increased by the ceremony and, in turn, nourishes the earth and the ancestral beings below, renewing their capacity to increase fertility and sustain life. On a topographical level, the surface pattern and colours of this work are not unlike the desert: the shimmering heat hazes and blistering heat, the subtle variations within its regularity and the sense of sameness.

52

Robert Ambrose Cole
Untitled

Robert Ambrose Cole
Untitled
1993
Plate 53

"I was born in Alice Springs. I paint my mother's and my father's country. My mother's country is Banka Banka, Warramunga people, north of Tennant Creek. Most of my paintings are from around Aputula Finke, my father's country. His country is south of Alice Springs, the sand hills on the edge of the Simpson Desert."[3]

Robert Cole is a young artist who is able to draw from the old and the new in Aboriginal culture, by virtue of his unique situation. He was educated in a white Australian environment, raised by traditional Aboriginal parents in urban Alice Springs and surrounded by the great desert art movement. As Cole himself has stated, his images "come from all over the place".

A self-taught artist, he began painting in 1988, while employed at the CAAMA (Central Australian Aboriginal Media Association) retail outlet in Alice Springs. During this period Cole worked closely with artists from the Utopia region. His paintings are contemporary interpretations of the design principles, characteristic of the region.

Using acrylic paint, Cole emulates the colours found in natural pigments. He explores the aesthetic potential of the traditional fluid use of dots to create an illusory chequer-board effect which is achieved by varying the size of the dots. There is also a sense of an aerial view of the land, whilst the subtle sand and saltbush tones infuse his paintings with a feeling for 'country'. In the second painting, the symmetrical flowing dots create a tension between the two red ochre boomerang shapes. These central forms also suggest the shape of a gorge, a deep natural fissure which occurs throughout the rugged ranges, rising dramatically from the

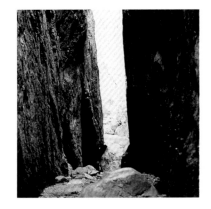

Stanley Chasm near Alice Springs.
Photo Christopher Hodges 1992

desert around Alice Springs. Like these significant features, the painting is charged with an intangible energy. The work is untitled and consciously abstract, in marked contrast to the narrative content of most works from this region.

The way this work unifies European abstraction and indigenous art into a personal view is increasingly common among young Aboriginal artists from towns and cities. Cole's work blurs the distinctions that segregate Aboriginal art practice into the increasingly redundant categories of 'traditional' and 'contemporary'. This work are fine expressions of the contemporary Aboriginal experience which draw on a range of cultural reference points, firmly rooted in the past and the present.

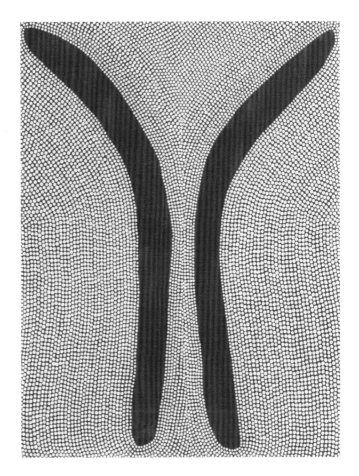

53

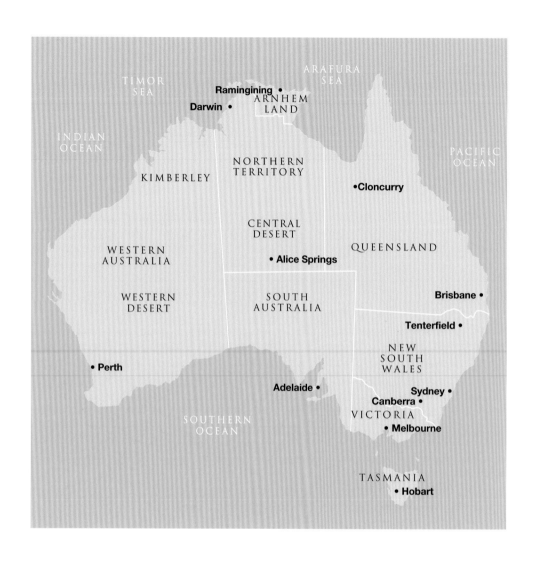

CLAIMING A SPACE

This section deals primarily with the contemporary experience of Aboriginal and Torres Strait Islander artists, living in towns and cities. Many of these artists are cultural activists in varying degrees, reclaiming their Aboriginal space after decades of displacement. Thus their works are political as well as cultural statements. Contemporary Aboriginal art from these sources appears more interventionist and challenging than the tradition-based styles. This is not to say that 'traditional' Aboriginal artists do not also use their art to convey political concerns, particularly over land issues. As early as 1963, the Yirrkala bark petition was presented to the Federal Government and a land rights series of bark paintings was produced by Central Arnhem Land artist David Malangi in 1983, one of which is included in this section.

By comparison, 'urban' styles are seen as "frequently audacious, unruly and disrespectful in ways unimaginable to traditional Aboriginal art and unanticipated by European avant-gardism".[1] In the process of referring to black and white cultures, artists from towns and cities are often obliged to satirise both cultures in order to drive home a point. The work of Richard Bell and Gordon Bennett exemplifies this aspect of the art now coming from towns and cities.

Though 'urban' forms of Aboriginal art deal directly with issues pertinent to their time and place, this does not rule out their drawing on the past. The Aboriginal past is often referred to through the use of cross-hatching, dotting or totemic images and other identifiable signs from traditional sources. The surface becomes an arena in which differences are reflected and some-times reconciled. Other artists draw on the past by interrogating the history written by the dominant culture. Artists like Rea, Judy Watson and Bronwyn Bancroft connect with a different version of Australian history in the process of re-writing their own private histories. Their work is often autobiographical and intensely personal, drawing on a range of media and genres, to communicate these journeys of self-exploration.

These works proclaim that Aboriginal art can be made on any surface, in any media, about subjects of relevance or concern – as it has always been.[2] It should not surprise anyone that Aboriginal and Torres Strait Islander art is changing as rapidly as the environment to which it is responding. This probably accounts for its dynamic and vital quality, so valued within contemporary art. The works in this section reflect a triple interplay between an ancient past, a complicated present and a white cultural milieu. This complex equation is a source of strength for these artists, in contrast to the disruption which similar conditions produced in the past.

The maturity and confidence, seen in these works, comes from their exploration of the territory between lessons of the past and the realities of the present, with an eye to the future. In the wider context of Australian society, they open up new ground, which must be settled in the continuing debate around reconciliation between black and white in this country. As Roberta 'Bobbi' Sykes wrote in 1984:

"Our creative people carry for us into the public arena the power of our healing process. They provide the vanguard of our relentless march towards justice, and depict for us the history of this march. Standing as they do, with one foot planted firmly in each world, their contribution to the art world, indeed to the entire world, is to fill a void regarding the Australianisation of this country's art."[3]

Ellen Jose
Life in the balance

"This bamboo construction based on the 'Nath' is used in the Torres Strait, for catching dugong. The shell which has many uses, also means 'Long Life'. So, I have the shell hanging in <u>Life in the balance</u> as part of the bamboo structure. The Globe represents how insignificant humans are in the universe. Although the earth seems to be teeming with life, in comparison to the age and extent of the Universe, life on earth can be equated with the first cell division after the moment of conception. All people from all cultures and religions and ages have grappled with the problem of existence. Some use science, space probes and radio telescopes to try to fathom their universe and use materials they are familiar with to create meaning and make sense of life..."

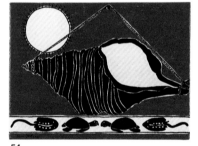

54

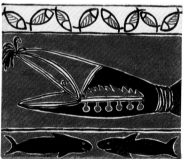

55

Ellen Jose is an artist of Torres Strait Island descent who has broken new ground by her innovative use of new technologies. In this work, Life in the balance, Jose has successfully fused symbols, objects and technology from her mixed heritage to expand indigenous expressions into more global arenas such as, concern for the environment. She has used the bamboo dugong trap, the bailer shell and the image of the shark drum from her Darnely, Horn and Murray Island traditions. From her European background comes the idea of installation art, watercolour painting and computer-generated images. The multi-media installation includes a 30 second video presentation as part of the work. The small watercolour entitled, Drum Beat is based on the shape of the shark, an important animal in the mythology of Jose's seafaring ancestors. The Water Container, showing the bailer shell suspended delicately in the air, suggests the fragility and tension of life in the balance.

A time when life was in balance is recalled through formal shapes and limited colours. Black, red and white are repeated throughout the pieces and there is a balance between two and three dimensional structures and between organic and geometric shapes.

The installation is a complex structure operating on many levels, consistent with the complexity of global issues and the intertextuality of much contemporary art. The dugong trap fits comfortably in its new context and functions like a clue to the solution of environmental abuse, suggesting that the answer may lie in our past.

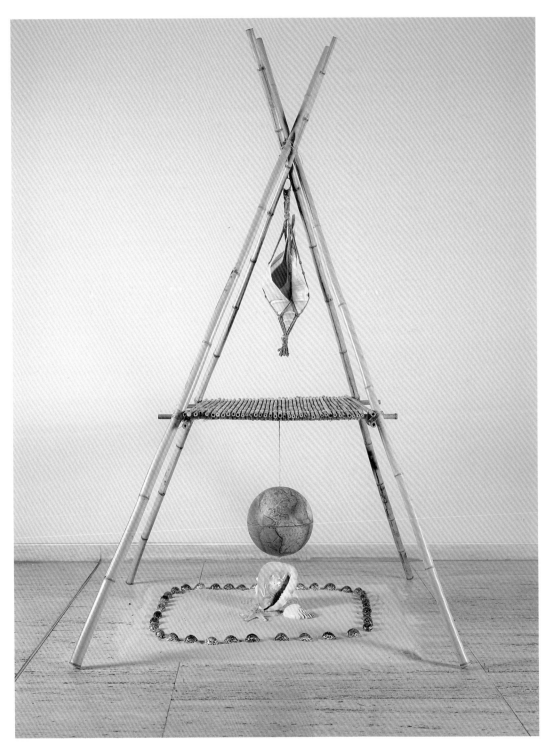

Lin Onus
Fruit Bats

"I have been regularly asked to which school or movement do I belong? Apart from some obvious responses... I guess that what I would have to say is that I belong to the Bower Bird School. You know the one – picking up bits and pieces, here and there..." [4]

Lin Onus picks up ideas from his Aboriginal heritage and the urban society he lives in, and works them together like a 'cultural mechanic'. He produces complex art works which challenge through humour. Painting since 1974, he is one of the pioneers of the 'urban' movement of Aboriginal artists and an important figure in contemporary Australian art.

The main focus of this sculptural installation is 100 fibreglass fruit bats suspended from a ready-made Hills Hoist clothes-line. The distinctive cross-hatched clan design (rarrk) from Arnhem Land painted on the bats instantly signals its Aboriginality. This humourous combination of the great Australian backyard icon 'the Hills Hoist', the bats and the surface decoration sets up a dialogue between the urban and traditional Aboriginal art styles in a contemporary art environment.

Onus would have encountered great flocks of roosting fruit bats in areas around the Arafura Swamp on his frequent visits to Central Arnhem Land. Their noisy squabbling and fluttering wings create a powerful kinetic presence ironically associated, in this piece, with the clothes which would normally be flapping from a clothes-line like this one. Instead, these brooding black shapes hang motionless in their artificial setting. The bat droppings that carpet the floor below refer to the droppings that surround particular roosting sites at certain times of the year. The floral design is based on the way bats, and the

ceremonial cycles associated with them, are depicted in bark and body painting and on hollow log coffins. These bats are important totems for the Ganalbingu clan whom Onus visits in Arnhem Land. The bark painting by David Malangi (see plate 41) is from the same area. The influence of art from this region can be seen in the markings on Onus' bats.

The tendency to whimsy, irony and humour is a powerful tool in Onus' work. It grabs attention, driving home messages about contradictions in black/white relations, but at the same time, demonstrating that working cross-culturally can create a harmonious whole. The work establishes a carefully balanced dialogue of sensory and conceptual elements, juggling the sacred and the mundane, the manufactured and the natural, old traditions with new technology and seducing the eye with teasing paradox.

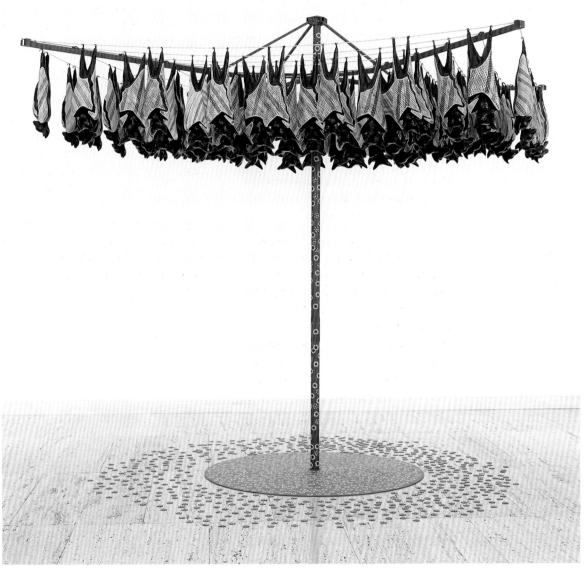

57

David Malangi
Abstract (River Mouth Map)

David Malangi
Abstract (River Mouth Map)
1983
Plate 58

Land rights affect all Aboriginal people and art has been used as a potent way of making political statements about these issues. Many traditional owners who have a continuous link with their land remain deeply concerned about the possibility that it might be leased to mining and fishing interests.

David Malangi lives at Yathalamarra in Central Arnhem Land and maintains strong cultural links with his land and heritage. He was invited to create and exhibit a group of works dealing with his land and Dreaming sites for Australian Perspecta 1983, a contemporary survey of Australian art held every two years at The Art Gallery of New South Wales. During discussions with the artist, at this time, he expressed concern for the protection of his Dreaming sites around the mouth of the Glyde River. The nine bark paintings completed subsequently became known as his 'land rights series'. Each painting maps part of Malangi's country like a 'deed of ownership'. They were shown, along with a conical mat and a conch shell, references to the Djang'kawu Sisters who created the country in ancestral times, demonstrating their religious function as well as their political one for the artist. The series travelled to the 1983 Sao Paolo Biennale, before being acquired by this Gallery.

"This is no ordinary place. This is my country... This is our traditional area and that is why we don't want any mining or balanda there... The river (where we are walking) is where our dreamings are. We have grown up with our culture and have kept it; our sacred sites, our ceremonies, and secret dreamings. My people and ancestors have lived here for a long time..." 5

Malangi has mapped an area at the mouth of the Glyde River at Dhamala, which he 'looks after'. It is a place where the Djang'kawu Sisters walked, creating Manharrngu country and naming all living things. It is also here that they had their sacred dilly bags containing their power stolen by the men, who from that time, became the controllers of ceremonies. The women retained the power to give birth and create new life. The many waterholes in the area were made by the Sisters plunging their digging sticks into the ground whilst moving about the country. After resting, they moved further west and created more Manharrngu country around Dhabila.

The diagram below left depicts the individual segments of the mouth of the Glyde River.

1 Garangala rock with Lungu
2 Raga nuts
3 Beach where Gunmirringu sat
4 Sea eagle tree
5 Mud skipper
6 Conch shell
7 Milmindjarrk waterhole
8 Bilma clapsticks
9 Dhona sacred digging stick
10 Catfish
11 Glyde River

The left side of the work represents the Eastern Bank and the right side, the Western Bank, where Dhabila and Dhamala are located.

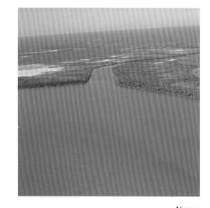

Above
Mouth of the Glyde River.
Photo Bulábula Arts Ramingining 1992

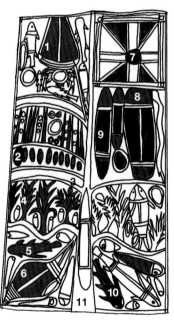

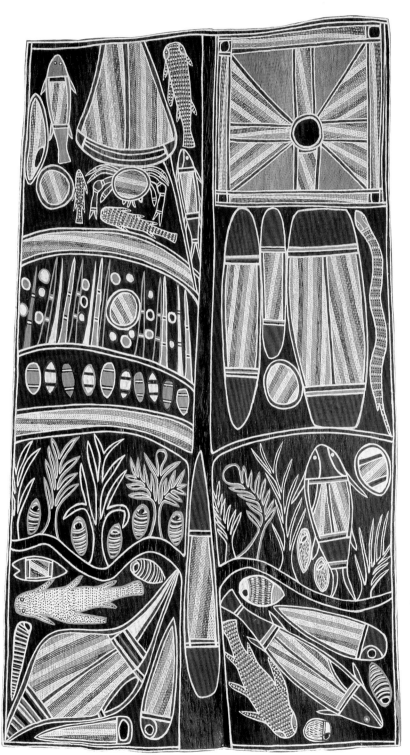

Mervyn Bishop
Prime Minister Gough Whitlam
pours soil into the hands of traditional Land
Owner Vincent Lingiari, Northern Territory

Mervyn Bishop
*Prime Minister Gough Whitlam
pours soil into the hands of
traditional Land Owner Vincent
Lingiari, Northern Territory*
1975
Plate 59

"I was the only Aboriginal press photographer in Sydney, in fact, Australia at that time (1964). The Herald had given me a break..."

Some 30 years later, Mervyn Bishop still retains the distinction of being the only Aboriginal press photographer in Australia. He came to prominence in 1971 when he won the Press Photographer of the Year Award. His photographic work in Aboriginal communities, (outside his duties as a press photographer) provide a valuable record, offering insights which it would be difficult, if not impossible, for a non-Aboriginal photographer to capture with such immediacy.

Access to photography provided Aboriginal people with an alternative way of seeing themselves. In the work of white photographers, they tended to appear as cultural curiosities: either noble savages or the demoralised remnants of a defeated race. Our sense of the importance of the moment and the significance of the symbolic gesture in this work is enhanced by the knowledge that the image was taken by an Aboriginal photographer.

On the 15 August 1975, Gough Whitlam picked up a handful of earth and poured it into the hands of Vincent Lingiari, an elder of the Gurindji people. This was a gesture of momentous significance, as it concluded the first successful Aboriginal land rights claim. Land at Wave Hill Station was handed back to the Gurindji people who are its traditional owners, after they had walked off the largest cattle station in Australia, owned by the London-based Vestey group.

After being employed as cheap labour for decades by Vestey's the Gurindji set up camp on their tribal land at Wattie Creek. The 'walk off' happened on 22 August, 1966 and lasted nine years.[6] The success of this action is regarded as a significant step in the beginning of a national movement which led to the landmark Mabo ruling of 1992, recognising Aboriginal peoples' prior ownership of the land.

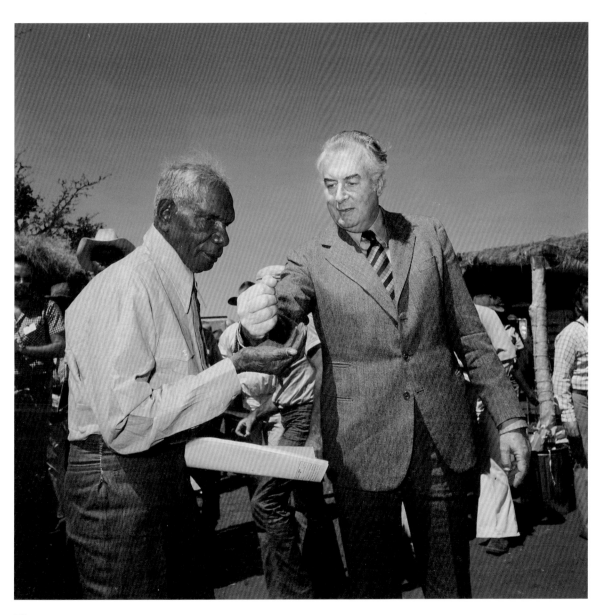

59

Gordon Bennett
Myth of the Western Man (White Man's Burden)

Gordon Bennett
Myth of the Western Man (White Man's Burden)
1992
Plate 60

"I use strategies of quotation and appropriation to produce what I call 'history' paintings. I draw on the iconographical paradigm of Australian, and by extension European, art in a way that constitutes a kind of ethnographic investigation of a Euro-Australian system of representation in general, but which has focused on the representation of Aboriginal people in particular... I wish to reinstate a sense of Aboriginal people within the culturally dominant system of representation... rather than as a visual sign that signifies the 'primitive' or 'noble savage' or some other European construct associated with black skin." [7]

Gordon Bennett began painting seriously in 1986, when he left his job at Telecom to study Fine Art. He did not learn about his Aboriginal heritage until he was 11 years old. He has stated that it took him the next 18 years to come to grips with its concealment. "My work is an attempt to come to grips with my own socialisation..."

In Myth of the Western Man (White Man's Burden) Bennett uses a web or overlay of 'Jackson Pollock' type paint on which are hung the dates of historical events that have shaped Australian national identity. These events are particularly, yet not exclusively, pertinent to New South Wales. At the centre of the painting, the figure of a European 'pioneer' spins around a pole, while these histories whirl around him. This figure appears in several of Bennett's paintings, and is taken from an illustration in a primary school text of an event in the 'narrative' of the Burke and Wills expedition. The pole signifies the dominant historical narrative of Western 'progress' and the British invaders' first act of colonising this land.

Bennett's work locates itself within the specific histories of Aboriginal and Euro-ethnic relations within Australia, questioning the prevailing accounts of these histories. It refers to their use as justification for historical and contemporary acts against Aboriginal people. Bennett's use of dots in most of his paintings draws on both traditional painting styles and the dot screen used in commercial printing, linking contemporary and European technologies. Bennett has adopted a strategy of reverse appropriation – taking images from European art and illustration – to counter the widespread appropriation of Aboriginal designs by non-Aboriginal people.

The artist provided the following timeline to accompany this 'history' painting:[8]

Key dates in the painting

1788   Colony established. Flag raised.

1795   1st legally sanctioned massacre of Aboriginal people – Hawkesbury River area – Troops sent from Parramatta.

1799   1st murder trial of five whites for the murder of two Aboriginal boys – found guilty, but released – pardoned three years later.

1802   Pemulwuy – killed and decapitated, his head sent to England.

1803   1st colony established in Tasmania.

1804   1st Massacre of Aborigines in Tasmania at Risdon Cove.

1813   Blaxland, Wentworth and Lawson cross the Blue Mountains into Wiradjuri land.

1824   Massacres of Wiradjuri people.

1838   Myall Creek Massacre in Northern NSW. 1st white man hung – against public opinion and in a retrial after acquittal in 1st trial – for the murder of Aborigines. This creates a climate of secrecy around further murders.

1857   Yeeman people (near Roma, Queensland) massacred.

1861   Largest massacre of whites by Aborigines in reprisal for hundreds of Aboriginal deaths – at Cullin-la-Ringo station, Queensland by the Kairi people.

1869   Tasmania – William Lanney – touted as the last male Aborigine – died. His grave is looted and skeleton stolen.

1876   Tasmania – Truganini dies – touted as the last Tasmanian Aborigine, her skeleton is put on display (against her last wishes) in the Tasmanian Museum.

1928   Coniston Massacre in the Northern Territory – near Yuendumu. Those responsible vindicated in an official (cover up) inquiry ending 7 February 1929.

1971   Yirrkala, Gove Peninsula – land rights thrown out of court.

1972   Aboriginal Tent Embassy set up in Canberra. Gough Whitlam elected and Blue Poles by Jackson Pollock purchased for Australia – (public outraged).

1976   Truganini's bones cremated and her ashes dispersed on the wind.

1992   Mabo Case is won – Terra Nullius is overturned.

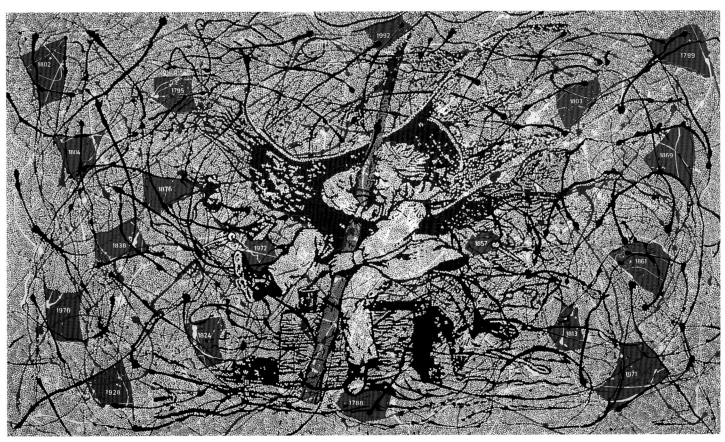

60

Richard Bell
Devine Inspiration

Right
Richard Bell
Devine Inspiration
1993
Plate 61

'Abos Blacks Coons Darkies Expecting Free Gifts Here In Justice Kindness Land Moderation Not Offered Peacefully Quickly Resourcefully Sincerely Tactfully Under Very Weak Xenophobic Yobbo Zookeepers'

This alphabetical sequence, which appears on Richard Bell's audacious work, is characteristic of his bristling good humour or as he calls it "intellectual terrorism". Bell confronts the dominant society with derogatory racist words that have been used to pigeon-hole Aboriginal people as inferior and only capable of living on hand-outs. This cultural stereotyping is reinforced by 'tourist images' of Aboriginal-identified boomerangs, snakes and hand prints which are often appropriated for use on tea towels and other marketable items, exploiting and demeaning the culture. At the same time, the practice of stencilling images onto rock walls evokes the ancient strength of Aboriginal culture. Bell characteristically signs his work with a small self-portrait, embedded in the bottom corner, which is also a proclamation of the artist's identity.

Devine Inspiration was inspired by a newspaper article entitled 'White guilt won't help black cause' written by Frank Devine in 1992 which challenged the underlying assumptions of the Royal Commission into Aboriginal Deaths in custody and called for a re-think about continued 'protection' of Aboriginal people through entrenched policies of 'apartheid'. However, Bell sees Devine as part of a "plethora of luminaries from the post-colonial Aryan ruling class who espouse their views on Mabo and indigenous people" and the Royal Commission itself as part of a 'whitewash' of the real problems to soothe their own guilt.[9]

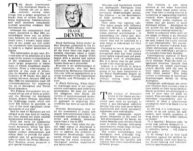

White guilt won't help black cause

A photocopy of Frank Devine's article accompanies Richard Bell's painting Devine Inspiration.

"I am a conduit for this radical Aboriginal view. 'Radical' being in terms of what white people see as radical. I don't see myself as radical. I've just stumbled across this art as something I can do. It's simply part of the process of knowing who you are as an Aboriginal person with the ability to paint, it's no big deal!... Our history has been sanitised and sterilised. I want to expose that, and the belief that says, if you tell a lie often enough it becomes a truth." [10]

Even in the rarefied atmosphere of the art world, Richard Bell's work gives no respite from the hard facts and home truths he forthrightly states. While much of the artist's work contains a keen sense of humour and irony, the sorrow and bitterness of the past is at the heart of it. Many of Bell's people – the Gamilaroi of northern New South Wales – were sent as far away as Palm Island as punishment for continuing to practice their traditions. Bell sees his art as a way of publicising the contemporary issues which face Aboriginal people and contradicts the stereotyped image of the Aboriginal person as a victim. His art is a celebration of cultural strength.

Described as "unashamedly propagandistic" by George Petelin in his catalogue essay for the Australian Perspecta 1993, Bell uses words like missiles, carefully selected to provoke guilt in the guilty. On other levels, he engages in art world debates about the 'white Aborigine' issue and appropriation raised by Imants Tillers, Juan Davila and other European-Australian artists.

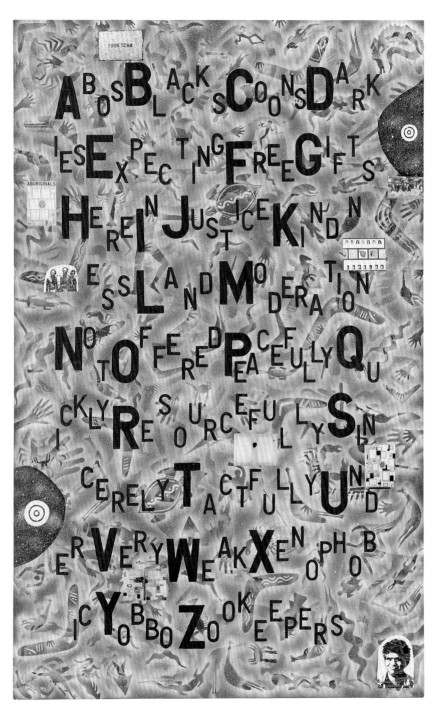

Harry J. Wedge
Stop and think

Harry J. Wedge
Stop and think
1993
(1 of 5 panels)
Plate 62

*"I try to paint what I dream: what I hear on
<u>A Current Affair</u>; things you can even hear people
talking about on the train..."*

Harry Wedge is both a social commentator
and a storyteller, chronicling his perceptions
about life with great candour. He draws on a
range of sources including childhood memories
of the Erambie mission near Cowra where
he grew up, observations of everyday life,
responses to current affairs programmes and
a concern about the cultural dislocation of
Aboriginal people.

The narratives Wedge tells through his
paintings, like those told by his ancestors, are
often didactic in nature, dealing with issues of
good and evil and emotions such as love, fear,
hate and anger. Wedge focuses on a particular
audience and 'goes for' their conscience without
mercy, but not without humour. His work tackles
current social and environmental issues like
pollution, alcohol and drug abuse and child
abduction as well as past injustices.

The five panelled Stop and think, is an
indigenous version of Little Red Riding Hood.
The threatened child is depicted as an emu
in green school uniform. The wolf – an imported
species – dressed in brightly-coloured clothing
symbolises the daily threat of evil affecting all
people while a little spirit hovers protectively
above.

A recurring and central presence in Wedge's
work is the spirit figure, which undergoes
metamorphosis from one painting to the next.
Representing both human and animal beings,
these figures are neither male nor female. With
their wild antennae of hair radiating from their
enlarged heads and their exaggerated eyes and
animal features, they have a close resemblance
to paintings of spirit figures found on rock walls
in northern New South Wales and Queensland. [11]

The stories that go with these images are an
integral part of Wedge's commentary. They are
spoken in the plainest language by the artist,
who neither reads nor writes. They have the
character of homespun tales passed from
generation to generation.

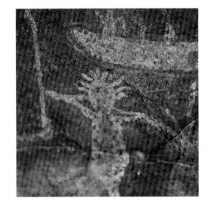

*Spirit Figures on cave walls
Laura, North Queensland.*

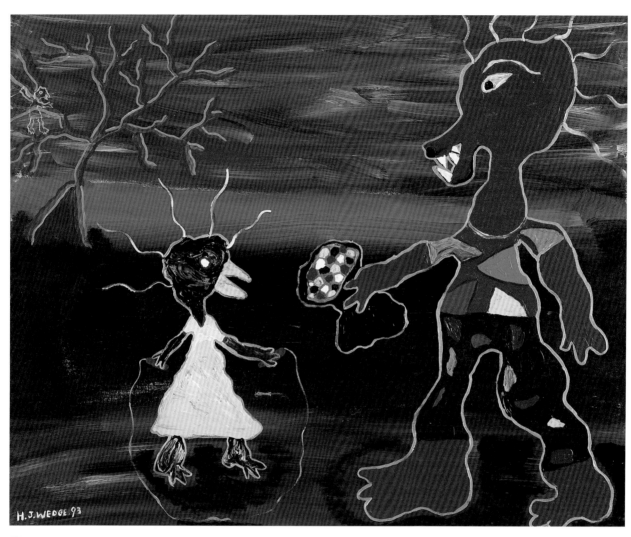

62

Bronwyn Bancroft
You don't even look Aboriginal

Bronwyn Bancroft
You don't even look Aboriginal
1991
Plate 63

"... for years we were punished for being black and now we are punished for not being black enough..."12

Bronwyn Bancroft, from the Tenterfield area in western New South Wales, is highly-regarded as an artist in textile design, painting and mixed media. Her work confronts issues affecting Aboriginal people from urban and rural areas. The artist's personal memories and associations involves her own interpretation of her Koori identity and the struggle of humanity to exist without destroying itself and our world.

You don't even look Aboriginal is Bancroft's response to an accusation that she and other Aboriginal people with light skin have to face almost daily, because their appearance does not conform to the cultural stereotype of a 'black' person. This view denies the events and changes of the past 200 years and displays an ignorance which insults many Aboriginal people. Bancroft reaffirms her Aboriginality by fusing a family tree structure with a genetic diagram that reaches back into her Aboriginal ancestry. Small circular passport photos of her forebears float in the genetic pool of the past, which borders on the inter-connected present in which Bancroft is pictured at various stages of her life:

"I think the genealogical statement across the top where my uncle, my grandmother, my aunty and my father are all listed is the reinforcement of my Aboriginal heritage in a way and they filter down. As a cross-section, the little twirling circle is indicative of my life with photographs taken over a period of 16 or 17 years and collaged together – so it's me at all different aspects of time. I used red and green to indicate black and white. It doesn't matter what colour you are... it matters that you know and believe in your family and heritage. So I used a river-like torrent to show that whatever pushes us through life, we should be allowed to be proud of our heritage."

The dynamic linear quality and sense of pattern associated with Bancroft's textile designs takes on a further cultural dimension in this work. Traditional motifs of circles, dots and overall surface patterning often found in desert art re-surface in a celebration of the life force. The upward thrusting form has a volcanic action in which the central 'lava flow', not only connects the artist with her past, but carries her into the future with a renewed sense of identity and vigour.

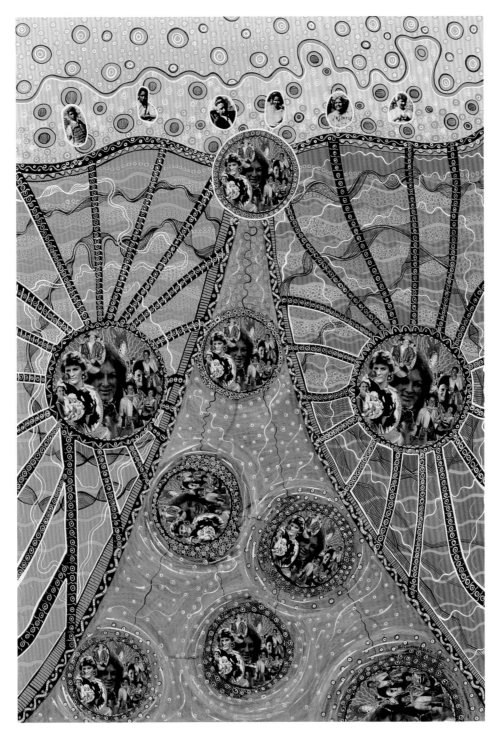

Rea
Highly Coloured – My life
is coloured by my colour

Rea
Highly coloured – My life is coloured by my colour
1993
(2 of 6 panels)
Plate 64

Rea, as she likes to be known, is a Gamilaroi woman from western New South Wales and works in Sydney. She is a photographer and computer artist who combines text, stylised colour motifs and photographic images to explore personal and cultural history.

A set of six colour images place the artist in the role of voyeur, with her camera pointed at the audience. These black and white, life-size self portraits of the artist, over-layed with a colour screen and text, rely on scale to confront the viewer on equal terms. Rea's work is about her identity as a black woman who, she feels, is seen as a member of a kind of invisible subspecies.

"These images are about parts of who I am, from my childhood to who I am now. In each one I am revealed in different ways, the orange is about when I was growing up as a child... I had to start with my mother, my major care giver... it is about when I was a kid and I had to ask 'Mum, can I have an orange?' The red is the gun at my head because that is how you feel when you are frustrated, angry and isolated. Purple and yellow are my mother's favourite colours and every house we went into, she always painted the kitchen purple and yellow. I gave the yellow colour to my Uncle, who died in custody because being my mother's brother he was closely related. I gave him yellow roses on his grave. He used to go and get orders from St Vinny's to feed us and clothe us. The blue and green is about growing up... the struggles and insecurity which is in the text and not separate from the image, 'Blue moon I saw you standing alone' and 'Green, I wish I could be seen.' "

The journey of self-discovery that Rea has embarked upon is about making herself more visible, but it is also a telling reversal of ethnographic practices in which the Aboriginal person is always the observed. The observed, in these works, becomes the observer. Rea sees the camera as her interface with the world and this is the way she wants it to see her. "With the colour screen, I can layer my memories and messages onto the solid black and white image. Colour photography is not what I am into, but colour is what I am into. Colour triggers my memories and feelings."

These works challenge the conventional European tradition of portraiture and the role this tradition has played in constructing images of Aboriginal people as a conquered race. As a set, these works function like a memory tableau in which each image can be seen as a single frame in an ongoing film process.

Yellow reminds me of the
roses which I put on my
Uncle's grave

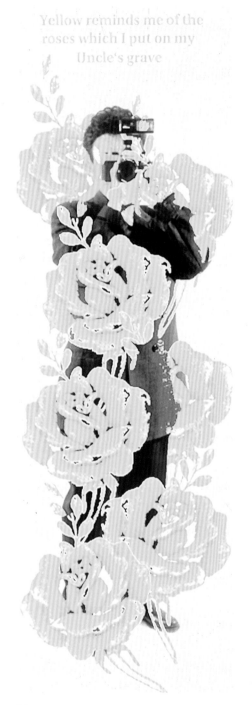

"MUM," SHE SAID "CAN I HAVE
AN ORANGE ?"

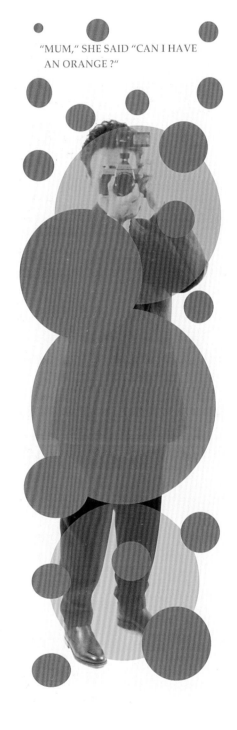

'Black to the Future' was the title of an article from the Sydney Morning Herald which marked the occasion of my appointment as Curator at The Art Gallery of New South Wales in 1994. For the first time, an Aboriginal person was in charge of an Aboriginal and Torres Strait Islander Art collection at a major public art gallery. It has taken a long time for such an appointment to be made and I see it as an important step and an indication of future directions. Aboriginal people need to say more about the way Aboriginal and Torres Strait Islander art is presented.

As the first Aboriginal person in this position, I believe there are many ways we could go. My own vision for Aboriginal art is that it be seen as Art and becomes fully-integrated with mainstream contemporary art. As an Aboriginal Curator, sensitive to community needs, deaccessioning and the return of special cultural works to their communities can also be more easily achieved. From time to time, as part of the reconciliation process, non-Aboriginal works will be shown along with Aboriginal works.

The new Aboriginal Gallery is named Yiribana which means 'this way' suggesting the direction for Aboriginal art and culture. My aim is to bring indigenous art alive in the Yiribana gallery and help to give the public a better understanding of its richness and diversity. As a Gamilaroi person, I am sensitive to the different concerns and expectations of the hundreds of other language groups across Australia. We plan to have up to six Aboriginal and Torres Strait Islander people working within the Aboriginal Art Department at The Art Gallery of New South Wales by 1995, some employed as special Aboriginal guides who will work with the existing guides. The Yiribana gallery will act as a cultural centre and keeping place. It will feature works from the permanent collection of The Art Gallery of New South Wales, small travelling exhibitions, storytelling and artists or performers-in-residence and cover events of importance to Aboriginal people.

The Art Gallery of New South Wales has been progressive in promoting Aboriginal and Torres Strait Islander people to positions where they can take control of their own art and culture. My hope is that other public galleries and museums in this country follow its lead.

Daphne Wallace
Curator of Aboriginal and
Torres Strait Islander Art

As Objects Conservator, my job is to work with my colleagues, the Curators and Registration staff to ensure that the Gallery's collection of Aboriginal and Torres Strait Islander art is preserved and displayed for the enjoyment and understanding of people now and in the future.

We use minimum intervention to preserve images. Emphasis is placed on preserving the original quality through understanding the nature of the materials used and employing handling methods and environmental controls.

Whilst it is tempting to criticise earlier attempts at preserving ephemeral objects like barks, if no treatment had been applied, more of the images would have been lost because of the inherent instability of unbound pigments on flexible bark surfaces. Each bark painting has its own particular form, yet it is flexible and likely to change in shape in response to humidity fluctuations. With handling, pigment flakes tend to pop off as the bark support is flexed. If the bark is restricted in its movement, it may split.

Bill Boustead, Senior Conservator at the Gallery from 1947 to 1977, has described some of his conservation methods. He used Bedacryl 122X, a polynbutyl methacrylate mixed with toulene (a highly toxic solvent) to consolidate friable pigments. He would spray the mixture onto the pigments, sometimes applying multiple coats. Boustead's notes record that he took care to avoid creating a shiny surface, but the soft powdery quality of the unbound pigments has been lost. White pigment has been obviously altered. This effect can also be seen on the Pukumani Poles, the 17 grave posts commissioned from the Tiwi people of Melville Island for the Gallery's collection in 1959. With only the resinous juice of mango leaves, crushed and mixed with water, rubbed onto the surface of the posts to act as a binder, consolidation was necessary (and probably applied in the 1970s) to prevent further loss of the decoration on the posts.

Attempts were also made to flatten barks on a vacuum hot table. The unpigmented side of the barks was coated with polyvinyl acetate emulsion during the flattening process in an attempt to prevent further dimensional changes. Holes were drilled in the corners of the bark paintings so flame-darkened copper wires could be threaded through to attach them to hessian covered masonite boards – or sometimes simply to nail the bark painting to the wall. It is no longer acceptable to drill holes in artefacts merely for display purposes, yet the perfect mounting method for barks has not been found.

Every owner/custodian of Aboriginal artefacts seems to have a different approach to display. Some artists lash sticks to the top and bottom of their bark paintings in an effort to keep them flat and to facilitate hanging. Other artists leave it to the purchaser to work out a hanging system. Nowadays, conservators favour display and transport mounting systems which provide overall support for the bark paintings. In the 1980s, individually designed supports made from fibreglass, polyester and casting plaster were used for this purpose. More recently, shaped aluminium grid supports have come into vogue, with plastic clips used to secure the bark painting to the support frame.

Curators must consider the aesthetics of display as an essential component of the presentation of works of art in an exhibition. Daphne Wallace, the Gallery's Curator of Aboriginal and Torres Strait Islander Art, prefers to see bark paintings floating on the wall with little obvious restriction from a mount. The frames in which bark paintings were previously exhibited the Gallery were distracting, although they did contribute to their preservation. The Gallery is trialling a modified aluminium support system which is visible at three points only. Particularly fragile barks will be displayed flat. The Curator and Conservator collaborate to ensure that the collection is exhibited appropriately in terms of both aesthetics and preservation.

Donna Midwinter
Objects Conservator, AGNSW

A conservator consolidates the original pigment on a bark painting.

Introduction

1 This is still the case in some areas of the international art world, John A McDonald, 'A snub for Aboriginal Art,' *Sydney Morning Herald,* August 6, 1994, p. 12

2 For a discussion on the reception of contemporary Aboriginal art see Marcia Langton, 'The two women looked back over their shoulders and lamented leaving the country: Detached comment (recent urban art) and symbolic narrative (traditional art)', *Art Monthly Australia* supplement, 1992-93, p. 9

3 For a discussion on the concepts of Aboriginality see Marcia Langton, 'Well I heard it on the Radio and I saw it on the Television...' *Australian Film Commission*, 1993, pp. 32 to 36

4 Hetti Perkins and Victoria Lynn, 'Blak Artists, Cultural Activists', *Australian Perspecta 1993, Biennial Survey of Contemporary Australian Art,* The Art Gallery of NSW, p. 10ff

5 See Ian McIntosh 'Maluku Totem Hunters and Sama-Bajau in North Australian Aboriginal Mythology' *Australia Folklore,* issue 10, 1994 presented at a seminar of the *Third International Maluku Research Conference,* Ambon, June 29, 1994. Also the activities of the Dutch-Portuguese and Japanese seafarers are seen in rock art and bark paintings.

6 A. Walker and R. Zorc, 'Austronesian Loan Words in Yolngu-Matha of North East Arnhem Land', *Aboriginal History,* vol 5, June 1981, pp. 109-134

7 There has been a phenomenal increase in the number of Aboriginal visual artists since the 1989 Department of Aboriginal Affairs Report of the Review Committee, *The Aboriginal Arts and Crafts Industry* (Australian Government Publishing Service Canberra, 1989) which put the figure at around 6,000. The Australia Council and the Aboriginal Artists' Biographical database at the Australian Institute of Aboriginal and Torres Strait Islander Studies suggest different figures. Estimates of the number of Aboriginal artists in Australia today vary enormously according to whether only artists who regularly sell their work through established arts organisations and galleries are included, or every Aboriginal person who claims to be an artist, regardless of the frequency of their output – or every Aboriginal person involved in any of the arts. Some figures also include Aboriginal people who only engage in art making in traditional ceremonial contexts.

History of a Collection

1 It is believed that these two sandstone carvings along with another called *Young Girl Waiting for her Lover* were purchased by Margaret Preston on one of her many trips to Queensland and the Northern Territory.

2 There had been earlier expeditions by anthropologists which included Baldwin Spencer, Gillen and Radcliffe-Browne in the early 1900s and Warner in the 1920s. See Spencer, W.B., *Native Tribes of the Northern Territory of Australia, 1914* and Lloyd Warner, W, *A Black Civilization – A Social Study of an Australian Tribe,* Harper and Brothers Publishers, University of Chicago, USA, Revised Edition 1958.

3 Exhibitions around this period included:

1949 Exhibition at David Jones Gallery, Sydney from part of large collection obtained in Arnhem Land by anthropologist, R. Berndt.

1951 Jubilee exhibition of Australian art – all capitals.

1957 Exhibition of Arnhem Land bark paintings and carved human figures held in Perth.

1957-8 Australian National Committee for UNESCO which prepared a display of Australian Aboriginal culture. This exhibition visited all states.

1960-1 Exhibition arranged by State Art Galleries of Australia which toured all states. Tony Tuckson was responsible for its organisation and presentation.

4 See Tony Tuckson, Notes *on the Collection,* The Art Gallery of NSW, 1959.

5 See Charles P Mountford, *Records of the American-Australian Scientific Expedition to Arnhem Land – Art Myth and Symbolism,* vol 1, Melbourne University Press, Melbourne 1948.

6 The largest share of the works from the AASEAL went to the Institute of Anatomy which has since become the National Museum of Australia, Canberra. They have recently been the subject of detailed research.

7 The remaining Port Keats (Wadeye) works were purchased in 1959 from the poet Roland Robinson who collected stories in the area in the early 1950s. Fourteen other works from this area came from Professor Harry Messel and from exhibition purchases.

8 Dorothy Bennett later came to pre-eminence as an avid collector and patron of Aboriginal art in Arnhem Land. She has lived in Darwin since 1960 and her knowledge and experience has been sought by many people since she first accompanied Dr Stuart Scougall on his trips into Arnhem Land from 1954.

9 The team arrived on Melville Island expecting to simply pack and freight the commissioned grave posts, only to find work had not commenced.

10 Adventurous in the context of the times. In 1988, the National Gallery of Australia acquired 200 log coffins from Central Arnhem Land, known as 'The Aboriginal Memorial' with curatorial assistance from Djon Mundine in his capacity as arts advisor at Ramingining.

11 Sali Herman chartered a plane from Darwin to Melville Island in 1959 soon after seeing the poles at The Art Gallery of New South Wales. This trip inspired a number of works, one of which is pictured. He then flew to Yirrkala and found the Tuckson team on their second collecting trip to the Northern Territory. Russell Drysdale visited Darwin and Melville Islands as early as 1956, subsequently returning many times. He was allowed to attend a pukumani ceremony and his experience became the source of the haunting Aboriginal subjects seen in his paintings at the his 1959 retrospective at The Art Gallery of NSW.

12 As recorded by Tony Tuckson in his essay, 'Aboriginal Art and the Western World', published in The Art Gallery of NSW, *Acquisitions Catalogue,* 1960.

13 Tuckson detailed information about the barks he collected and published in The Art Gallery of NSW, *Acquisitions Catalogue,* 1959. Dorothy Bennett documented the works purchased by Dr Scougall, most of which became part of this collection.

14 Interview with Dorothy Bennett, 15 July 1994. This led to Scougall's publication *One Stance in the Aborigines,* Halstead Press, Sydney, c1960s

15 Dr Scougall often took Australian artists and others involved in the arts with him on these trips. They included Russell Drysdale, Michael Campbell, Rudi Komon and Hal Missingham, the then Director of The Art Gallery of NSW.

16 See David H Bennett, 'Malangi :The Man who was Forgotten before he was Remembered', *Aboriginal History,* vol 4, issue 1, 1980.

17 The space was designed by an architect from the Government Architect's Office and named the Captain Cook wing.

18 It appears that the only state art gallery actively purchasing desert art during the 1970s was museums and art galleries of the Northern Territory. Some museums, including the South Australian Museum and the Australian Museum in Sydney, purchased a few works from Papunya Tula in the mid to late 1970s.

19 This era refers to the period Labor came into power with Gough Whitlam as Prime Minister. He immediately set about implementing Labor's Aboriginal Policy which included the protection of Aboriginal land against uranium mining in the Northern Territory. This and a range of other reforms gave Aboriginal people more say in their own affairs and helped to create the social confidence expressed in the artistic growth of the past two decades.

20 See *Australian Perspecta 1981: Biennial Survey of Contemporary Australian Art,* The Art Gallery of NSW. One of the works included in *Perspecta 1981* was *Warlugulong* by Clifford Possum and Tim Leura Tjapaltjarri which was purchased for the collection. The first sand mosaics ever to be seen outside Central Australia were constructed in the grounds of the S. H. Ervin Gallery on Observatory Hill by artists of the Papunya Tula company in January 1981 during the Festival of Sydney. The event was offered to the Gallery but space was not available.

21 Interview, August 11, 1994 with Terence Maloon at The Art Gallery of NSW.

22 Most art institutions did not collect Western Desert Art before the 1980s.

23 *Australian Perspecta 1983: a Biennial Survey of Contemporary Australian Art,* The Art Gallery of NSW, p. 15

24 Daphne Wallace is the first full-time permanent Aboriginal curator to head a department of Aboriginal art in the country. Hetti Perkins from Boomalli Aboriginal Artists Cooperative was a guest curator and curated Aboriginal shows and assisted with other curatorial tasks at The Art Gallery of NSW.

25 Nine barks from this series were the first Aboriginal works to be included in a contemporary Australian art exhibition and catalogue at a major gallery. Bernice Murphy the curator of *Australian Perspecta 1983* commissioned these works, thereby opening new doors for Aboriginal art.

26 After his untimely death in 1973 at the age of 52, Margaret Tuckson suggested to Tony's friends that they may like to visit the *Pukumani Grave Posts* and think of Tony. He did not have a church service and this was considered a more meaningful alternative.

A Collection Begins

1   Margaret Preston, 'From Eggs to Electrolux', *Art in Australia*, third series, no 22, December, 1927

2   Preston was probably the first publicly to recognise aesthetic qualities in Aboriginal art. Only six articles were published on Aboriginal art between 1916 to 1942 in *Art in Australia*. Four were written by Preston (1925, 1930, 1940 and 1941) and the other two by anthropologists, Ursula McConnel in 1935 and Fred McCarthy in 1939.

3   A description applied to the works of Kalboori Youngi, an Aboriginal woman from Queensland whose works bear a striking resemblance to these pieces. See Sutton, Peter ed., *Dreamings: The Art of Aboriginal Australia*, Viking in association with The Asia Society Galleries, New York, 1989, p. 199. David Kaus at the National Museum of Australia is of the opinion that it is possible that Kalboori Youngi, Linda Craigie and Craigie Lee may be the same person. It is also possible that they may have worked either closely together or were at least familiar with each others' work.

4   According to Ian McIntosh of the Northern Territory University, recent anthropological studies have shown that the complex mythology and history associated with this group of outsiders is based around perceived inequalities between Aboriginal people and early Macassans. He suggests that at the 'beginning of time', Aboriginal people were fair-skinned and 'rich technologically', and that the darker-skinned Macassans worked for them. The Dreaming narratives indicate that through misadventure this situation was reversed. So, while the stories of the Bayini sometimes refer to early Macassans they are also seen as the original Aborigines, thus accounting for their easy acceptance into Aboriginal society. This may also help to explain why the Bayini are considered to be a separate group to the Macassans.

Land Before Time

1   Personal corrospondence with Kim Akerman, August, 1994.

2   This artist is recently deceased (1993). As a mark of respect his name should not be said aloud in accordance with Aboriginal laws governing the mourning period. The new name used to refer to this artist is Lilipiyana.

3   Jennifer Isaacs, *Aboriginality: Contemporary Aboriginal paintings and prints,* University of Queensland Press, 1989, p. 76

4   McGillick, Paul, 'Much more than trendy art', *Financial Review*, Friday, May 17, 1991

5   Ulli Beier, *Dream Time – Machine Time: the art of Trevor Nickolls*, Aboriginal Artists Gallery, North Sydney, 1985, p. 26

6   Beier, p. 28

Land Maps

1   Sutton, p. 18

2   See Vivien Johnson, The *Art of Clifford Possum Tjapaltjarri,* Gordon and Breach Arts International, Sydney 1994, p. 47ff. Johnson describes Clifford Possum as 'a cartographer of the Dreaming' and discusses the complexity of the mapping procedures.

3   Johnson, p. 54

4   Johnson, p. 142

5   Jane Hardy, J. V. S. Megaw and Ruth M. Megaw, The *Heritage of Albert Namatjira: the watercolourist of Central Australia*, William Heinemann, Port Melbourne, 1992, p. 287. Quote by Jillian Namatjira, grand-daughter of Albert Namatjira.

6   Hardy, Megaw and Megaw, p. 268

7   Christopher Hodges in *Australian Perspecta 1993: a Biennial Survey of Contemporary Australian Art,* The Art Gallery of NSW, p. 82

8   Ryan, Judith, 'Images of Dislocation: Art of Fitzroy Crossing' in Judith Ryan, and Kim Akerman, *Images of Power: Aboriginal Art of the Kimberley*, National Gallery of Victoria, Melbourne, 1993, p. 64

Sorry Business

1   Tony Tuckson accompanied by his wife Margaret, Dr Scougall and Dorothy Bennett arrived on Melville Island to supervise the shipment of the commissioned *Grave Posts* to Sydney, but were surprised to find that the work had not commenced. However, it was a fortuitous oversight, as it gave the team the opportunity to document the production of the Grave Posts over the following two weeks. It was an extraordinary effort, for the five artists to produce seventeen poles of such size and quality in that time.

2   These grave markers are not to be confused with the Aboriginal log coffins produced in Arnhem Land, which contain the remains of the deceased.

3   Jennifer Hoff, *Tiwi Grave Posts,* National Gallery of Victoria, Melbourne, 1988, p. 24

4   Malangi and his people with the assistance of the Northern Territory Sacred Sites Authority and the Northern Land Council worked together to keep commercial fishermen out of this officially 'closed' area.

5   Malangi transcripts, from Bulábula Arts.

6   David H Bennett, 'Malangi: The Man who was Forgotten before he was Remembered', *Aboriginal History,* vol. 4, no.1, 1980, 43-47. For details of the controversy surrounding the alleged unauthorised use of the design (see also *History of a Collection* in this book).

7   A total of 40 sandstone carvings were donated by Dr Ronald and Mrs Alison Fine and Dr Gordon Davies.

8   See section notes in *A Collection Begins*.

Shimmer

1   Contrary to popular assumptions the extensive use of dots in Aboriginal art did not originate with the desert art movement in the 1970s.

2   Wititj is a generic name which refers to the various manifestations of the Great Serpent related to the Wagilag Sisters' cycle. Terms used to refer to this creative being vary between regions and interpretations of the cycle. Sometimes he is a serpent, other times a python or a particular snake as in this case.

3   From Christopher Hodges, Sydney, 1993.

Claiming a Space

1   George Petelin writing on Richard Bell in *Australian Perspecta 1993*, The Art Gallery NSW, p. 20

2   Traditional artists have always used whatever surfaces were available for artistic mark making: bark, bodies, tree trunks, rocks, woven objects, nuts, seeds, egg shells and later paper and canvas. A similar variety of pigments and tools were employed.

3   *Koori Art '84,* exhibition catalogue, Artspace, Sydney. Nearly ten years later another exhibition, entitled *Commitments* which toured from September 1993 to July 1994, addressed the issue of reconciliation. Through a process of negotiation, black and white artists worked collaboratively on pieces which address historic imbalances in artistic and political representation.

4   Lin Onus, Artist's Statement, Gallery Gabrielle Pizzi, Melbourne, 1991.

5   David Malangi, *Australian Perspecta 1983,* The Art Gallery of NSW, p. 67

6   Three years prior to the 'walk out' in 1966 the people of Yirrkala in north eastern Arnhem Land took a petition written on bark in the Gumatj language to Federal Parliament to protest against the leasing of their land to the Swiss mining company Nabalco. Although this case was lost in the Supreme Court, on the grounds that under Australian law they had no title to the land, the Yirrkala bark petition was the first land claim to be pursued in the courts.

7   Gordon Bennett, in the catalogue accompanying his solo exhibition at the Contemporary Art Centre, South Australia, 1993.

8   Most dates and information gleaned by Gordon Bennett from *Blood on the Wattle: Massacres and Maltreatment of Australian Aborigines since 1788* by Bruce Elder, Child and Associates, Sydney, 1988

9   The article by Frank Devine appeared in *The Australian,* March 13, 1992.

10   From *True Colours, Aboriginal and Torres Strait Islander artists raise the flag*, Boomalli Aboriginal Artists Co-operative, 1994.

11   Harry Wedge disclaims knowledge of these rock spirit images despite the resemblance. The reappearance of images in successive generations from different regions testifies to the persistence of Aboriginality through art.

12   Bronwyn Bancroft. Address at the reception for *Recent and Future Acquisitions*, The Art Gallery of NSW, July 5, 1993.

It should be recognised that skin names are not like European surnames (of Vivien Johnson's, Aboriginal Artists of the Western Desert - A Biographical Dictionary, notes on the biography, pp. 51-56). For the purposes of this publication artists have been indexed alphabetically by last name.

Artist unknown
Emu c1960
Milingimbi, Central Arnhem Land, N.T.
Paperbark, vegetable fibre string, beeswax, feathers, natural pigments
54.6 x 7.6 cm (at base)
Purchased 1962

Artist unknown
Pukumani Grave Post (Tutini) 1958
Snake Bay, Melville Island, N.T.
Natural pigments on wood
165.1 x 29.2 cm
Gift of Dr Stuart Scougall 1959

Artist unknown
Bark Basket 1958
Snake Bay, Melville Island, N.T.
Natural pigments on bark, fibre string
40.7 x 1 7.8 x 33.1 cm
Gift of Dr Stuart Scougall 1959

Artist unknown
Map of Groote Eylandt c1948
Groote Eylandt, N.T.
Natural pigments on bark
94.0 x 57.1 cm
Purchased 1959

Artist unknown
The Wild Honey, Koko 1948
Milingimbi, Central Arnhem Land, N.T.
Natural pigments on paper
58.1 x 45.7 cm
Gift of the Commonwealth Government 1956

Artist unknown
Bayini, men and women of Port Bradshaw 1948
Yirrkala, North East Arnhem Land, N.T.
Natural pigments on paper
46.0 x 58.7 cm
Gift of the Commonwealth Government 1956

Artist unknown
The Rainbow Serpent Narama and her sons 1948
Liverpool River, West Arnhem Land, N.T.
Natural pigments on paper
45.7 x 58.4 cm
Gift of the Commonwealth Government 1956

Artist Unknown
Harbour Bridge 1939
La Perouse, NSW
Cardboard, blue velvet and assorted shells
9.0 x 17.0 x 5.0 cm
Gift of Alan Lloyd 1994

Bronwyn Bancroft Born 1958
Language group: Bundjalung
You don't even look Aboriginal 1991
Grafton, New South Wales
Gouache, collage on paper
120.0 x 90.0 cm
Mollie Gowing Acquisition Fund for Contemporary Aboriginal Art 1993
Born in Tenterfield, NSW, Bundjalung artist Bronwyn Bancroft is represented in major galleries in Australia and overseas. As a painter, her work has been exhibited both nationally and internationally in many group exhibitions and several solo shows. She is a founding member of Boomalli Aboriginal Artists Cooperative in Sydney, established in 1987. Bancroft has been widely known as a textile designer. Her shop Designer Aboriginals ran successfully from 1985 to 1990 selling fabrics and fashions and training Koori women in design. She has illustrated several books and was awarded a Creative Artist Fellowship from the Australia Council.

Don Baruk-madjua
Language Group: Tiwi
Pukumani Grave Post (Tutini) 1958
Snake Bay, Melville Island, N.T.
Natural pigments on wood
184.5 x 21.6 cm
Gift of Dr Stuart Scougall 1959

Richard Bell Born 1953
Language Group: Gamilaroi
Devine Inspiration 1992
Brisbane, QLD
6 photographic panels on composition board
244.0 x 153.0 cm
Purchased 1993
Richard Bell was born in Charleville. He now lives and works in Brisbane and has become a prominent contemporary artist since he started exhibiting in 1992. His work has been collected by major national and state galleries in Australia and he has been the recipient of a number of prestigious commissions and fellowships winning the Gold Coast Conrad Jupiter's Art Award in 1993.

Gordon Bennett Born 1955
Myth of the Western Man (White Man's Burden) 1992
Brisbane, QLD
Synthetic polymer paint on canvas
175.0 x 304.0 cm
Purchased 1993
Gordon Bennett was born in Monto, Queensland and now lives in Brisbane. By 1989 he had his first solo exhibition in Brisbane, and won the prestigious Moet & Chandon Australian Art Fellowship in 1991

Birari
Language Group: Murrinpatha
Creation of Five Waterholes 1961
Port Keats (Wadeye), N.T.
Natural pigments on bark
120.6 x 99.0 cm
Gift of Dr Stuart Scougall 1961

Mervyn Bishop Born 1945
Prime Minister Gough Whitlam pours soil into the hands of traditional land owner Vincent Lingiari N.T. 1975
Sydney, NSW
Cibachrome photograph
image 30.7 x 30.5 cm
Hallmark Cards Australian Photography Collection Fund 1991
Mervyn Bishop was born in Brewarrina, New South Wales. His move to Sydney in 1963 was the beginning of a celebrated career which included a four year cadetship with the Sydney Morning Herald, and later the News Photographer of the Year award, unprecedented achievements for an Aboriginal person at that time. He also worked as the first public relations photographer for the newly created Department of Aboriginal Affairs in Canberra in 1974. As a trained adult education teacher, he has passed his knowledge and experience on to other young Aboriginal students. His work is represented in major galleries and museums in Australia and has toured internationally.

Nym Bunduk 1900-1974
Kevin Bunduk Born 1942
Language Group: Murrinpatha
Emus Feeding c 1960
Port Keats (Wadeye), N.T.
Natural pigments on bark
179.0 x 78.8 cm
Gift of Dr Stuart Scougall 1961

Linda Craigie
Two Ladies Waiting c1940
QLD
Sandstone carving
13.5 x 12.8 x 4.0 cm
Gift of Margaret Preston 1948

Robert Cole Born 1959
Untitled (2 works) 1993
Alice Springs, N.T.
Synthetic polymer paint on canvas
140.0 x 110.0 cm
Purchased Mollie Gowing Acquisition Fund for Contemporary Aboriginal Art 1993
Robert Cole grew up and was educated in 'The Gap', the Aboriginal end of Alice Springs, and later worked in the CAAMA (Central Australian Aboriginal Media Association) shop. Self-taught, he began painting in 1988, influenced by the imagery passing through the shop, and also drawing on stories from his people.

Dawidi Djulwarak 1921-1970
Language Group: Liyagalawumirri
Wagilag Sisters' Story c1960
Milingimbi, Central Arnhem Land, N.T.
Natural pigments on bark
73.0 x 38.1 cm
Gift of Dr Scougall 1960
Dawidi lived in the Milingimbi area in Central Arnhem Land. He was a very important ritual leader and prolific artist. He is brother to Dawarangulili who also painted variations of the Wagilag theme. Some years after his death in 1970 the rights to paint the narrative in Dawidi's style were passed on to his daughter

Daisy Manybunhurrawuy and husband Joe Djembungu. Many of the Liyagalawumirri designs Dawidi used had died with him.

John Dodo Born 1910
Language Group: Karadjeri
Maparn (Doctor Man) c1985
La Grange, Eighty Mile Beach, W.A.
Natural pigments on carved sandstone
35.5 x 1 4.0 x 21.0 cm
Gift of Dr Ronald and Mrs Alison Fine
John Dodo at La Grange, south of Broome in Western Australia. He lives at the Bidyadanga community in the same area where he has been carving for the past twenty years with the encouragement of Lord McAlpine who held a large collection of his works. The Aboriginal Arts Board, the Museum of Western Australia and the Department of Anthropology in Western Australia have recently purchased his carvings. He has long been a skilful carver of finely engraved wooden objects and pearl shells.

Micky Dorrng Born c1950
Language Group: Liyagawumirr
Djang'kawu Sisters' at Gariyak 1993
Howard Island, Central Arnhem Land, N.T.
Synthetic polymer paint on canvas
1985.0 x 1350.0 cm
Purchased 1994
Micky Dorrng was born at Gariyak, located on the mainland bordering the Hutchinson Straits in 1946. His access to the knowledge of both the Liyagawumirr and Garrawurra people enable him to paint important stories. He had his first solo exhibition in Melbourne in 1991 and is represented in the National Gallery of Australia, The Art Gallery of New South Wales and the USA.

Bob-One Gala-ding-wama
Language Group: Tiwi
Pukumani Grave Post (Tutini) 1958
Snake Bay, Melville Island, N.T.
Natural pigments on wood
200.6 x 21.6 cm
Gift of Dr Stuart Scougall 1959

Mathew Gilbert Born c1920
Language Group: Yawuru.
Head c1985
La Grange, Eighty Mile Beach, W.A.
Natural pigments on carved sandstone
41.0 x 18.0 x 16.0 cm
Gift of Dr Ronald and Alison Fine
Born in the bush near Broome sometime in the early 1920s, Mathew's age is not recorded. He started making heads in the 1980s, following the example of John Dodo who was selling heads to Lord Alistair McAlpine.

Philip Gudthaykudthay Born 1935
Language Group: Liyagalawumurri
Badurru (hollow log coffin) and Dindin (wooden Mindirr) 1985
Ramingining, Central Arnhem Land, N.T.
Wood, natural pigments
29.0 x 15.0 x 14.0 cm
Purchased 1985
Philip Gudthaykudthay was born at Mulgurrum.

He was initiated around 1949, at Gatji creek near present day Ramingining. He was adopted by a Murrungun family after the death of his parents. He has had two solo exhibitions in Sydney, in 1983 and 1991, and has participated in numerous group exhibitions since 1980. His work is represented in all state galleries and in the National Gallery of Australia.

Gungiambi (attributed)
Untitled c1960
Milingimbi, Central Arnhem, N.T.
Natural pigments on bark
57.5 x 23.2 cm
Gift of Dr Stuart Scougall 1960

Ellen Jose Born 1951
Life in the Balance 1993
Melbourne, VIC
Bamboo, sand, shell, string, globe and rope
260.0 x 170.0 x 170.0 cm
Purchased 1993
Ellen Jose was born in Cairns and obtained professional qualifications in art and education from colleges in Brisbane and Melbourne. She has exhibited extensively over the last 8 years in solo and group exhibitions nationally and internationally. She works in a range of media including wood block printing and computer graphics, the first indigenous women to do so. She is represented in the major national and state galleries in Australia and a number of state libraries and universities.

Katy Kemarre Born c1945
Language Group: Alyawarre
Female figure 1993
Ngkawenyerre, Utopia, N.T.
Synthetic polymer paint and wool on wood
142.0 x 19.0 x 17.0 cm
Purchased 1994
Katy lives at a soakage at Ngkawenyerre near Utopia. She has been exhibiting in group exhibitions with other Utopia artists since the late 1970s. Once a batik painter she now works on canvas and carves in wood. Her work is about her country and associated women's ceremonies. Katy's work is represented in national and private collections.

Emily Kame Kngwarreye Born c1910
Language Group: Anmatyerre
Untitled 1992
Utopia Soakage, Central Desert, N.T.
Synthetic polymer paint on canvas
165.0 x 480.0 cm
Purchased Mollie Gowing Acquistion Fund for Contemporary Aboriginal Art 1992
Emily Kame Kngwarreye was born on a soakage called Alalgura on what was once Utopia Station. She is one of Australia's leading contemporary artists and the first Aboriginal visual artist to receive an Australian Artist's Creative Fellowship from the Prime Minister in 1992. Her work has received wide critical acclaim and is collected in major public and private collections in Australia and overseas.

Crusoe Kurdal Born 1964
Language Group: Kunwinjku
Mimi Figures 1985

Maningrida, West Arnhem Land, N.T.
Wood and natural pigments
266.0 x 25.0, 272.0 x 15.0, 270.0 x 14.0 cm
Purchased 1985

Charlie Quiet Kwangdini
Language Group: Tiwi
Pukumani Grave Post (Tituni) 1958
Snake Bay, Melville Island, N.T.
Natural pigments on wood
149.8 x 26.8 cm
Gift of Dr Stuart Scougall 1959

Paddy Lilipiyana c1920-1993
Language Group: Liyagalawumirri
Paddy was the custodian of the Wagilag religous story which he inherited from Dawidi. His was a celebrated bark painter who was most active in the 1960s and whose work has been widely collected.

Dorothy Djukulul Born 1942
Language Group: Ganalbingu
Wagilag Sisters' Story: Wurrutjarra-sand palm 1989
Ramingining, Central Arnhem Land, N.T.
Natural pigments and synthetic polymer paint on bark
108.0 x 63.0 cm
Purchased 1989
Dorothy was born at Mulgurrum, near Ramingining, Central Arnhem Land. She is one of a small handful of women bark painters who were taught by their fathers and/or uncles in the 1960s. Her skill was much admired and she was encouraged to continue. She exhibited jointly with her husband Djardi Ashley in Melbourne in 1983 and performed at the Sydney Biennale in 1986. Since then she has exhibited in group shows in a number of cities and is represented in the National Gallery and other major galleries as well as in the Robert Holmes A Court collection.

David Malangi Born 1927
Language Group; Manharrngu
Gunmirringu funeral scene 1983
Milingimbi, Central Arnhem Land, N.T.
Natural pigments on bark
156.5 x 74.0 cm
Purchased 1984
Abstract (River Mouth Map) 1983
Ramingining, Central Arnhem Land, N.T.
Natural pigments on bark
135.0 x 78.0 cm
Purchased 1984
David Malangi was born into the Manharrngu clan at Mulanga, near the mouth of the Glyde River Central Arnhem Land. He has been painting on bark commercially for over thirty years and before that on the bodies of deceased kinsmen, performers and hollow log coffins. In 1979 he was one of three artists from Ramingining selected to exhibit in the Biennale of Sydney. This was the first time Aboriginal artists had exhibited at this level. He is well-known for his Gunmirringu funeral paintings, one of which appeared on the Australian one dollar note in 1966 and was the subject of con-troversy. In 1983 his land rights series of barks also drew attention here in the Australian

Persecta show and at the Biennale in Sao Paulo. In 1988 he was instrumental in the creation and installation at the Sydney Biennale of the 200 log coffins known as the Aboriginal Memorial to mark 200 years since European invasion. He has been invited to exhibit and attend seminars here and overseas. He lives at Yathalamarra, near Ramingining with his wives and children and actively pursues his painting and ceremoni-al activities.

Mangudji Born 1909
Language Group: Gunavidji
Man with Leprosy c 1959
Oenpelli, Western Arnhem Land, N.T.
Natural pigments on bark
75.0 x 39.7
Gift of Dr Stuart Scougall 1961

Mau
Language group: Djabu
The Morning Star Ceremony c1960
North East Arnhem Land, N.T.
Natural pigments on bark
120.6 x 64.2 cm
Gift of Dr Stuart Scougall 1960

Mawalan Marika 1908-1967
Language Group: Rirratjingu
Figure of Ancestral Being of the Dhuwa moiety 1960
Yirrkala, North East Arnhem Land, N.T.
Feathers, bark and paint on wood
76.0 x 10.0 x 14.0 cm
Gift of Dr Stuart Scougall 1960
Djang'kawu Creation Story 1959
Yirrkala, North East Arnhem Land, N.T.
Natural pigments on bark
188.0 x 64.8 cm
Gift of Dr Stuart Scougall 1959
Mawalan Marika was born at Yirrkala. He was from the Dhuwa moiety. He is the father of other well-known artists, Wandjuk, Banduk, Bayngul and Dhuwarrwarr. Amongst his many achievements as a master painter is a mural he painted for the Yirrkala Church about Dhuwa moiety religious cycles, now in the Buku-Larrnggay Arts Museum, Yirrlkala.

Mawalan 1908-1967
assisted by Wandjuk, Mathaman, and Woreimo Marika
Language Group: Rirratjingu
Djang'kawu story (no. 1) 1959
Yirrkala, North East Arnhem Land, N.T.
Natural pigments on bark
191.8 x 69.8 cm
Gift of Dr Stuart Scougall 1959

Gurruwiwi Midinari 1929-1976
Language Group; Gurruwiwi
Djaykung- File snakes c1960
Yirrkala, North East Arnhem Land, N.T.
Natural pigments on bark
280.0 x 70.0 cm
Gift of Harry Messel 1987
Midinari was born in Ngaypinyu near Blue Mud Bay. He is from the Galpu clan and was a prolific artist until his death in 1976. His work was distinguished by a skilful use of surface patterning and a concentration on the Wagilag

religious cycle. He was the sole inheritor of the rights to use the dot design on the body of the Great Serpent, Wititj. His work has been collected by all major institutions and a number of private collectors in the 1960s and 1970s. Karel Kupka collected some notable early works for the Sorbonne in Paris. The work pictured in this book was recently part of the large exhibition called Aratjara - Art of the First Australians *which toured Europe.*

Ginger Riley Munduwalawala Born c1937
Language Group: Mara
Limmen Bight River Country 1992
Ngukurr, Limmen Bight, N.T.
Acrylic on canvas
244.0 x 244.0 cm
Purchased 1992
Ginger Riley Mundawalawala was born at Ngukurr. His meteoric rise is attested to by the numerous exhibitions, awards and attention his work has received here and overseas, since he first exhibited in 1989. His work is represented in all major galleries and collections in Australia as well in the Australian Embassy in Beijing. He won the National Aboriginal and Torres Strait Islander Heritage Art Award and the Patrick McCaughey Award in 1993.

Spider Nabunu/Mulumirr c1924-c1970
Language Group: Dangbon
Long-necked tortoise 1956
Beswick Creek, West Arnhem Land, N.T.
Natural pigments on bark
80.7 x 48.3 cm
Gift of Dr Stuart Scougall 1960

Jimmy Nakkurridjidjlma c1917-1982
Language Group: Kunwinkju
Mamalait, the starving children c1961
Oenpelli, West Arnhem Land, N.T.
Natural pigments on bark
59.7 x 101.6 cm
Gift of Dr Stuart Scougall 1961

Albert Namatjira 1902-1959
Language Group: Aranda
Palm Valley 1940s
Hermannsburg, Central Desert, N.T.
Watercolour on paper
37.0 x 54.0 cm
Purchased 1986
Albert Namatjira was born west of Alice Springs. He grew up on a Lutheran Mission at Hermannsburg away from his family. In the 1930s he changed from making wooden poker work to European style watercolour painting learnt from the artist Rex Batterbee. His first solo exhibition in 1938 made him a celebrity and he gained citizenship a decade before other Aboriginal people in 1957. However despite the media attention, he lived a life of frustrating con-tradictions. He was refused a grazing lease over his own land, yet required to pay taxes, given full citizenship and permitted to drink alcohol but imprisoned for sharing it with his countrymen. He died in 1959 disillusioned with white society. However, he was instrumental in giving impetus to the desert art movement we see today.

Fred Nanganharralil 1938-1993
Language Group: Djambarrpuyngu
Darrpa, King Brown Snake c1986
Milingimbi, Central Arnhem, N.T.
Natural pigments on bark
152.5 x 72.7 cm
Purchased 1988
Fred Nanganharralil was born at Gurrala in the Buckingham Bay area of Central Arnhem Land. He is from the Djambarrpuyngu language group and lives near Ramingining. The images he paints, such as the bailer shell tracks and the King Brown snake, relate to the Wagilag cycle. He also paints the Morning Star story and his mother's country. His work is held in the National Gallery of Australia and other state collections.

Mitjili Napurrula Born c1930
Language Group: Pintupi
Untitled 1993
Haasts Bluff, N.T.
Synthetic polymer paint on canvas
56.0 x 76.0 cm
Purchased 1994
Mitjili was born at Haasts Bluff. She started painting for sale in 1993 and exhibited at the Gallery Gabrielle Pizzi, Melbourne in 1994.

Nora Nathan
Emu Egg Hunting c1940
QLD
Sandsone carving, coloured with natural pigments
13.0 x 27.0 x 7.0 cm
Gift of Margaret Preston 1948

Nicholas
Language Group: Mayall
Spirit figure in the form of a skeleton c1960
Beswick Creek, West Arnhem Land, N.T.
Natural pigments on bark
55.2 x 34.3 cm
Purchased 1960

Trevor Nickolls Born 1949
The Garden of Eden 1982
Adelaide, S.A.
Synthetic polymer paint on canvas
121.5 x 121.5 cm
Purchased with funds donated by Sir Ronald Brierley 1992
Trevor Nickolls was born in Port Adelaide, South Australia to an Aboriginal mother and a white father. He was educated at art schools in Adelaide, Canberra and Melbourne and has maintained a full-time professional career as an artist for twenty years. He has a Diploma of Fine Arts and is a qualified art teacher. He has recieved a number of significant awards and grants including a creative arts fellowship at the Australian National University. He was also one of two artists selected to represent Australia at the Venice Biennale in 1990 (the other was Rover Thomas from the Kimberley) and his work as represented in Aratjara - Art of the First Australians which toured Europe in 1994. He is also represented in all major collections in Australia with a growing representation overseas.

Jimmy Njiminjuma Born 1945
Language Group: Kunwinjku
Yawk Yawk 1985
Maningrida, West Arnhem Land, N.T.
Natural pigments on bark
49.0 x 26.0 cm
Purchased in 1985
Jimmy lives in West Arnhem Land and spends a lot of time on his outstation at Mumeka with his family. He is well-known for painting the Rainbow Serpents, Namarrkon, Ngalyod and Yingarna as well as Yawk Yawk, the water spirits. His is a highly respected bark painter whose work is widely represented in all major collections in Australia and overseas.

Lin Onus Born 1948
Language Group: Yorta Yorta
Fruit Bats 1991
Mebourne, VIC
100 fibreglass polychromed fruit bats, Hills hoist, polychromed wooden disks
250.0 x 250.0 x 250.0 cm
Purchased 1993
Lin Onus was born in Melbourne, his mother was from Glasgow and his father was Aboriginal from Cummeragunja, near Echuca. He is a self-taught artist and has exhibited widely across the continent. He has held numerous one man shows and his work is represented in many important collections. He has won many awards, received prestigious commissions and undertaken a number of residencies including one in Japan and toured Aboriginal art and culture internationally. He has held significant positions on Aboriginal arts management and funding bodies including chairperson of the Aboriginal Arts Unit of the Australia Council.

Ada Bird Petyarre Born c1930
Language Group: Anmatyerre
Awelye for the Mountain Devil Lizard 1993
Mosquito Bore, Utopia, N.T.
Synthetic polymer paint on polycotton
180.0 x 205.0 cm
Mollie Gowing Acquisition Fund for Contempoarary Aboriginal Art 1994
Ada Petyarre lives and works near what was once Utopia Station approximately 250 kms north-east of Alice Springs. This is the traditional land of the Anmatyerre and Alyawarre peoples, which was bought back from a white landowner in 1978. The Utopia people now live in a series of family camps in the area. Ada has been exhibiting in group exhibitions since 1977, first as a distinguished batik artist and later as a painter on canvas. Her works have been extensively acquired in national as well as international collections.

Rea Born 1962
Language Group: Gamilaroi
Highly Coloured – My life is coloured by my colour 1993-94
Sydney, NSW
Computer generated photographs
180.0 x 100.0 cm (two from a set of six)
Purchased with funds provided by the Young Friends of The Art Gallery Society of NSW 1994
Rea was born in Coonabarabran in western

New South Wales. *She studied Visual Arts at the College of Fine Arts and at the Eora Centre in Sydney after doing a year as an apprentice electrician. She had her first solo exhibition in 1994 and has participated in a number of group exhibitions over the past three years. She has a number of awards and is represented in two state museums and some smaller collections. Her professional activities include lecturing and curating exhibitions*

Rover Thomas Born 1926
Language Group: Kukaja/Wangajungka
Ngarin Janu Country 1988
Warmun, W.A.
Ground pigments in synthetic polymer resin on canvas
100.0 x 140.0 cm
Purchased 1988
Rover Thomas was born in the area of the Great Sandy Desert in Western Australia. He spent most of his life in the Kimberley region where he worked as a stockman. It was in 1975, when he moved to Turkey Creek, that a major revelation occurred as a result of the accidental death of a relative and the Darwin cyclone. The visitation by the spirit of the dead woman transformed his life and the art of the region. He started exhibiting in 1987 and is represented in the collections of all major Australian galleries and has shown in 26 exhibitions, including the Venice Biennial, 1990 He received the Patrick McCaughey Prize in 1990 and has had work reproduced on a one dollar stamp.

Ronnie Tjampitjinpa Born c1943
Language Group: Pintupi
Untitled 1994
Kintore, Western Desert, N.T.
Synthetic polymer paint on linen
183.0 x 152.0 cm
Purchased 1994
Ronnie Tjampitjinpa was born into the Pintupi language group, west of the Kintore Range in Western Australia, around 1940. His family originally came in from the bush at Yuendumu. Ronnie later moved to Papunya iand now lives and works at Kintore in the Northern Territory. He won the Alice Springs Art Prize in 1988 and had his first solo exhibition at the Gabrielle Pizzi Gallery in Melbourne in 1989 followed by one at Utopia Art in Sydney in 1994. His work is represented in major art collections in Australia as well as in Paris.

Clifford Possum Tjapaltjarri Born 1932
Tim Leura Tjapaltjarri 1939-1984
Language Group: Anmatyerre/Aranda
Warlugulong 1976
Papunya, Central Desert, N.T.
Synthetic polymer paint on canvas
168.5 x 170.5 cm
Purchased 1981
Clifford Possum Tjapaltjarri was born in a creek bed some 200 kilometres north-west of Alice Springs. He grew up in the heyday of the cattle industry in the thirties and forties around Napperby Station. He is fully initiated into traditional life and started his artistic career at eighteen as a carver. In the 1950s he

was offered an opportunity to work in watercolours with Albert Namatjira but declined. He won the Alice Springs Art Prize in 1983 and is represented in all major galleries and collections in Australia. His work is well known internationally after being shown in France, Germany, USA, London, Brazil and New Zealand.

Willy Tjungarrayi Born c1930
Language Group: PIntupi
Tingari Story 1986
Kintore, Western Desert, N.T.
Synthetic polymer paint on linen
360.0 x 240.0 cm
Purchased 1993
Willy Tjungarrayi was born at Patjantja, southwest of Lake McDonald in the Northern Territory, deep in Pintupi country. His family made the journey hundreds of kilometres east to Haasts Bluff by camel in the 1950s. He later moved to Papunya and now lives at Kintore. During the 1980s he exhibited in numerous Papunya Tula shows in Melbourne, Sydney and Brisbane. Along with other other Papunya artists toured America and Europe in 1983, and the United Kingdom in 1987. His work is held in major public and private collections in Australia.

Laurie Nelson Tuki-al-ila
Language Group: Tiwi
Pukumani Grave post (Tutini) 1958
Snake Bay, Melville Island, N.T.
Natural pigments on wood
243.8 x 28.0 cm
Gift of Dr Stuart Scougall 1959

Samuel Wagbara Born 1928
Language Group: Maung
Three Mimi Dancing c1964
Croker Island, West Arnhem Land, N.T.
Natural pigments on bark
76.2 x 54.6 cm
Purchased 1964

Cory Surpise Wakartu Born c1929
Language Group: Walmajarri
Jijli 1991
Fitzroy Crossing, W.A.
Synthetic polymer paint on paper
56.0 x 76.0 cm
Purchased 1992
Cory Surprise was removed from her country of Pilmarr in the Great Sandy Desert along with the rest of her people when she was a child. She lived and worked at Christmas Creek Station before moving to Fitzroy Crossing where she started painted at the Karrayili Education Centre. Her work is now promoted through Mangkaja Arts Resource Centre and is attracting attention from major galleries. Cory has been involved in three group shows since 1991- in Adelaide, Sydney and Melbourne.

Judy Watson Born 1959
Language Group: Waanji
the guardians, guardian spirit 1986/87
Sydney, NSW
Powder pigment on plywood
180.0 x 58.0 cm

Purchased 1990
Inside the rock 1988
Sydney, NSW
Powder paint, oil paint, bitumen, charcoal
and oil stick on canvas
19.8 x 128.0 cm
Purchased 1990
She was born in Mundubbera, Queensland. She is a descendent of the Waanji people from the South West Gulf of Carpentaria. Judy Watson is a multi-media artist whose work is distinctly powerful and innovative. She was artist-in-residence at The Art Gallery of NSW in 1993. Although she is urban based and educated with an art school background, much of her work refers back to the land and its totemic spirit. She is a trained printmaker and painter, but works across many areas in pursuit of her expressive goals. Her first solo exhibition was held in 1986 and she has been involved in multiple group shows since 1979, including ones in New York and India. A recipient of numerous awards and grants, her work is well represented in all major collecting institutions as well as universities, corporate collections and the Tokyo National University of Technology.

H. J. Wedge Born 1957
Language Group: Wiradjuri
Stop and think 1993
Sydney, NSW
Synthetic polymer paint on canvas
100.0 x 100.0 cm (one of a set of five)
Purchased 1994
H. J. Wedge was born at Erambie Mission, Cowra in New South Wales. He worked as a drover, and fruit picker until a chance meeting led him to study photography at the Eora Centre, Sydney in 1989. Painting became his preferred medium and he had his first solo exhibition in 1991. This was followed rapidly by a regular succession of solo and group shows as well as an award a grant and some commissions including a CD cover for the band Midnight Oil. Despite his relatively recent arrival on the professional art scene his fresh look at indigenous and other issues has already resulted in his work being collected by the NGV and NGA as well and a number of smaller collections.

Attributed to Jabarrgwa (Kneepad) Wurrabadalumba
Language Group: Bara
1896 (deceased)
Dugong Hunt 1948
Groote Eylandt, North East Arnhem Land, N.T.
Natural pigments on bark
45.7 x 96.5 cm
Gift of the Commonwealth Government 1956

Attributed to Manggangina Wurramara
Language Group: Wanungwadarrbalangwa
Dumabiyandangwa kestrel 1948
Groote Eylandt, North East Arnhem Land, N.T.
Natural pigments on bark
40.7 x 68.7 cm

Gift of the Commonwealth Government 1956

Anchor Barrbuwa Wurrkidj Born 1924
Language Group: Kunwinkju
Mimi Hunter and Corroboree c1965
Oenpelli, West Arnhem Land, N.T.
Natural pigments on bark
71.1 x 48.3 cm
Gift of Dr Stuart Scougall 1966

Big Jack Yarunga
Language Group: Tiwi
Pukumani Grave Post (Tutini) 1958
Snake Bay, Melville Island, N.T.
Natural pigments on wood
210.8 x 27.9 cm
Gift of Dr Stuart Scougall 1959

Plate 1
Macassan Prau c1948

Plate 2
Sydney Harbour Bridge 1939

Plate 3
Barama and Lany'tjung – Yirritja Creation c1960

Plate 4
Two Ladies Waiting c1940

Plate 5
Emu Egg Hunting c1940

Plate 6
The Kestrel 1948

Plate 7
Bayini, men and women of Port Bradshaw 1948

Plate 8
Dugong Hunt 1948

Plate 10
The Rainbow Serpent Narama and her sons c1948

Plate 9
The Wild Honey, Koko 1948

Plate 11
Long-necked tortoise c1956

Plate 12
Mamalait, the starving children c1961

Plate 13
Man who had leprosy 1961

Plate 14
Djang'kawu Myth (no. 1) 1959

Plate 15
Ancestral Figure of the Dhuwa moiety 1959

Plate 16
Djang'kawu Creation Story 1959

Plate 17
Djang'kawu Sisters at Gariyak 1994

Plate 18
Wagilag Sisters' myth 1960

Plate 19
The Wagilag Sisters' Story: Wurrutjurra – Sand Palm 1989

Plate 20
Garden of Eden 1982-84

Plate 21
Limmen Bight Country 1992

Plate 22
Mimi Figures 1985

Plate 23
Three Mimis Dancing 1964

Plate 24
Mimi Hunter and Corroboree c1961

Plate 25
Yawk Yawk 1985

Plate 26
Inside the rock 1988

Plate 27
Spirit in the form of a skeleton 1960

Plate 28
the guardians, guardian spirit 1986/1987

Plate 29
A map of Groote Eylandt c1948

Plate 30
Warlugulong 1976

Plate 31
Palm Valley 1940

Plate 32
Untitled 1994

Plate 33
Tingari Story 1986

Plate 34
Jilji 1991

Plate 35
Ngarin Janu Country 1988

Plate 36
Emus Feeding 1961

Plate 36
The Creation of Five Waterholes c1961

Plate 38
Pukumani Grave Posts, Melville Island 1958

Plate 39
Hollow Log Coffin and Dilly Bag 1985

Plate 40
The Morning Star Ceremony 1960

Plate 41
Gunmirringu funeral scene 1983

Plate 42
Gunmirringu the great hunter 1983

Plate 43
Head 1985

Plate 44
Maparn (Doctor Man) 1985

Plate 45
Djaykung – File Snakes c1960

Plate 46
Darrpa, King Brown Snake c1986

Plate 47
Emu c1956

Plate 48
Untitled c1956

Plate 49
Untitled 1992

Plate 50
Female Figure 1993

Plate 51
Awelye for the Mountain Devil Lizard 1994

Plate 52
Spears at Ualki 1993

Plate 53
Untitled 1993

Plate 54
Water Container 1993

Plate 55
Drum Beat 1993

Plate 56
Life in the balance 1993

Plate 57
Fruit Bats 1991

Plate 58
Abstract (River Mouth Map) 1983

Plate 59
Prime Minister Gough Whitlam pours soil into the hands of traditional Land Owner Vincent Lingiari, Northern Territory 1975

Plate 60
Myth of the Western Man (White Man's Burden) 1992

Plate 61
Devine Inspiration 1993

Plate 62
Stop and think 1993 (1 of 5 panels)

Plate 63
You don't even look Aboriginal 1991

Plate 64
Highly coloured – My life is coloured by my colour 1993 (2 of 6 panels)

Primary Sources

Margaret Preston Papers, The Art Gallery of NSW Library

Tony Tuckson Papers, The Art Gallery of NSW Library

Information sourced from:
Kim Akerman
Dorothy Bennett
Edward I Ierman
David Kaus
Nigel Lendon
Fred McCarthy
Mary Macha
Terence Maloon
Peter Sutton
Margaret Tuckson

Tuckson, Tony, Sketchbook from Melville Island

Tuckson, Tony, Notebook from Yirrkala visit

Trustees Minutes, The Art Gallery of NSW, 1948

Secondary Sources

Artist's files and documentation accompanying art acquistions, The Art Gallery of NSW, 1949-1966

Akerman, Kim and McKelson, Fr Kevin, Kimberley Sculpture by Big John Dodo catalogue of a Touring Exhibition sponsored by the Australian City Properties Limited, 1989

Aratjara Art of the First Australians Traditional and Contemporary works by Aboriginal and Torres Strait Islander artists, Kunstsammlung Nordhein-Westfalen, Düsseldorf, Bernhard Lüthe and the Aboriginal Arts Unit of the Australia Council, Sydney 1993

Aboriginal Womens Exhibition, The Art Gallery of NSW catalogue 1991

Australian Bureau of Statistics, Census of the Australian Population 1971, Census of the Australian Population 1991

Arnhem Land Dreaming Bark Paintings from the Tasmanian Collections, Tasmanian Museum and Art Gallery

Australian Perspecta 1981: A Biennial Survey of Contemporary Australian Art, The Art Gallery of NSW

Australian Perspecta1991: A Biennial Survey of Contemporary Australian Art, The Art Gallery of NSW

Australian Perspecta 1993: A Biennial Survey of Contemporary Australian Art, The Art Gallery of NSW

Beier, Ulli, Dream Time - Machine Time: the art of Trevor Nickolls, Aboriginal Artists Agency, North Sydney 1985

Bennett, David H., 'Malangi:The Man who was Forgotton before he was Remembered,' Aboriginal History, vol. 4, no. 1, 1980

Butel, Elizabeth, Margaret Preston: The Art of Constant Re-arrangement (Viking in conjunction with The Art Gallery of NSW, Sydney 1985)

Caruana, Wally, Aboriginal Art, Thames & Hudson, New York 1993

Departmental files with particular reference to interpretative label texts by Hetti Perkins on artists Wedge, Bell, Cole and Bennett. The Art Gallery of NSW.

Department of Aboriginal Affairs 'Report of the Review Committee',The Aboriginal Arts and Crafts Industry, Australian Government Printing Service, Canberra, 1989

Diggins, Lauraine ed., A Myriad of Dreaming: Twentieth Century Aboriginal Art, Malakoff Fine Art Press, Melbourne 1989

Goddard, R. H., 'Aboriginal Sculpture', ANZAAS Report, XX1V, 1939

Johnson, Vivien, The Art of Clifford Possum Tjapaltjarri, Craftsman House, Sydney and Gordon and Breach Arts International,1994

Johnson, Vivien, Aboriginal Artists of the Western Desert – A Biographical Dictionary, Craftsman House, Sydney, 1994

Kerr, Joan ed., Heritage: The National Women's Art Book, Fine Arts Press, Roseville (forthcoming 1995)

Hardy Jane, Megaw, J.V.S. and Megaw, M. Ruth, The Heritage of Namatjira the watercolourist of Central Australia, William Heinemann, Port Melbourne 1992

Hoff, Jennifer, Tiwi Graveposts National Gallery of Victoria, Melbourne 1988

Hoff, Jennifer and Taylor, Luke, 'The Mimi Spirit as Sculpture', Art in Australia, 23 (1), 1985-6

Isaacs, Jennifer, Aboriginality: Contemporary Aboriginal Paintings and Prints, University of Queensland Press, Queensland 1989

McGillick, Paul, 'Much more than Trendy Art', Financial Review, Friday, May 17, 1991

McIntosh, Ian, Who are the Bayini? A seminar presented at the University of the Northern Territory, 12 August 1994.

Macknight CC, The Voyage to Marege, Melbourne University Press, Melbourne 1976

Mirritji, Jack, My People's Life – An Aboriginal's own story, Literature Production Centre, Milingimbi, N.T. 1976

Morphy, Howard, 'From dull to brilliant: the aesthetics of spiritual power among the Yolngu', Man, 24, 1, 1989

Mountford, Charles P, Records of the Australian-American Scientific Expedition to Arnhem Land, vol 1, Melbourne 1948

O'Ferrall, Michael O, Keepers of the Secret: Aboriginal Art from Arnhem Land, The Art Gallery of Western Australia, Perth 1990

Preston, Margaret, 'From Eggs to Electrolux', Art in Australia, third series, no. 22, December 1927

Ryan, Judith 'Images of Dislocation: Art of Fitzroy Crossing' in Ryan, Judith and Akerman, Kim, Images of Power Aboriginal Art of the Kimberley, National Gallery of Victoria, Melbourne 1993

Sutton, Peter ed., Dreamings: The Art of Aboriginal Australia, Viking in Association with The Asia Society Galleries, New York, 1988

Taylor, Luke, 'The Rainbow Serpent as a Visual Metaphor in Western Arnhem Land', Oceania, vol. 60, no.4, June 1990

Tillers, Imants, 'Intervening Devices, Some Reflections on the Post-Modern Landscape', A paper delivered at the National Gallery of Australia Conference entitled On the Line: Re-hanging Ausralian Art, July 1994

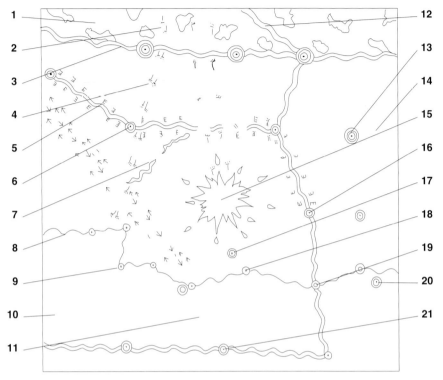

Taken from Johnson Vivien, *The Art of Chifford Possum Tjapaltjarri*, Craftsman House, Sydney 1994.

Warlugulong 1976

1 Sandhill lined clay pan lake country, home of a Great Snake
2 Lungkata's Blue Tongue Lizard sons forced back by the fire
3 Travelling route of Yarapiri, the Great Snake from Wlnparku
4 Dancing Women from Pikilyi
5 Upambura, Old Possum man travels back home to Napperby
6 **Kerrinyarra**
7 Two Carpet Snakes travel north-easterly from the clay pan lake
8 **Takarilla-Buntjia**
9 Pair of Carpet Snakes travel the country, holding ceremonies
10 Mala Hare Wallaby men travel in a fighting group, armed with spears
11 Emu from Yaliyumu travelling to Walpiri country

12 Storm from Kalipinpa which formed the Rain Dreaming
13 Wedge-tailed Eagle kills Euro at Wakulpa
14 Women travelling from Aileron area for ceremonies
15 **Warlugulong**
16 Mala Hare Wallaby men and Possum men have a big fight, the northern Possum men having a great advantage because they possess boomerangs (as well as spears)
17 **Kutupa**
18 **Aruakuna**
19 **Arangkia**
20 Euro begins frantic attempt to escape attacking Wedge-tailed Eagle
21 Takara

The use of images

In many Aboriginal communities the use of images of the deceased is suppressed until the end of the mourning period. Care has been taken to exclude such images from this publication and those included have been cleared with the relevant communities. Similarly, all other images and information have been cleared for publication. To the best of the author's knowledge no restricted material has been included in this book.

The spelling of Aboriginal words

In the absence of a standardised orthography of Aboriginal languages in Australia the spellings used are those preferred by respective communities at the time of publication. Spellings are constantly changing between regions and within single language groups depending on current linguistics. An attempt has been made to standardise spellings in this book except in cases where historic accuracy requires otherwise.

The use of select terms

Koori is the word generally used by Aboriginal people from the south-eastern corner of the continent generally describe themselves. In Queensland the word is **Murri**, in South Australia, **Nunga**, and in Western Australia, **Nyoongah**. In traditional societies, people use the name of their clan or language in addition to the word **Yolgnu** which is used in most parts of Arnhem Land.

Balanda – A term used by Aboriginal people in Arnhem Land to refer to white people or Europeans. It is believed to be a corruption of the word 'Hollander' from the Dutch who were visiting the north coast of Australia for centuries before European settlement.

Moiety – An anthropological term that simply means "half", and signifies a ritual division of creation into complementary halves, rather like the Asian concept of Yin and Yang. It determines marriage laws and social relationships as well as property and ceremonial rights and responsibilities.

Acknowledgements

Thanks to Kim Akerman, Museum of the Northern Territory, Darwin; Kate Alport, the South Australian Museum; Dr Jon Altman, Australian National University; Bulábula Arts; Boomalli Aboriginal Artists Co-operative; Renee Free, Deborah Edwards, Terence Maloon, Barry Pearce, Ursula Prunster, The Art Gallery of NSW; Christopher Hodges, Utopia Art, Sydney; Dr Jennifer Hoff; Rex and Ruth Iredale; Dr Vivien Johnson; David Kaus, National Museum of Australia; Dr Joan Kerr, University of NSW; Kate Khan, The Australian Museum, Sydney; Beverley Knight, Alcaston House Gallery, Melbourne; Nigel Lendon, Canberra School of Art; Lisa Mackay-Sim; Ian McIntosh, N.T. University; Dr Betty Meehan, Australian Hertitage Commission; Bernice Murphy, Museum of Contemporary Art, Sydney; Jodi Neale; Gael Newton, National Gallery of Australia; Dr Barry Russell, Northern Territory Museum of Arts and Sciences; Luke Taylor, National Museum of Australia; Daniel Thomas; Peter Sutton; Dr Sue-Anne Wallace, National Gallery of Australia; Neville White; Yaja.

I am indebted to Tony Tuckson, Charles Mountford, Dr Stuart Scougall and Dorothy Bennett for the details they recorded in the 1940s and 1950s. Sections in this book are based on their documentation. Bulábula Arts in Ramingining, Northern Territory have been extremely helpful in providing information, maps and images on the bark collection.

Margaret Tuckson must be acknowledged for the many photographs she took at Yirrkala during 1959.

Interpretations of art works included are based on information received from artists in various forms or from communities in the case of the deceased.

I owe a great personal debt to Jack Mirritji, a Djinang man from Warngibimirri, Central Arnhem Land. Over many years we developed a deep bond, out of which grew a desire to exchange our different cultural and personal experiences.

I would like to thank the photography and design departments at The Art Gallery of NSW.

Current Benefactor
Mollie Gowing

Major gifts over 10 pieces
The Commonwealth Government – 24 (collected by Charles Mountford)

Dr Stuart Scougall – 181
Professor Harry Messel – 38
Dr Ronald and Mrs Alison Fine – 27
Dr Gordon Davies – 13

Other donors
Margaret Tuckson
Marjorie Gartrell
Joan Grimmond
Renee and Keith Free
Mollie Gowing
Allan Mashford